Marketing the IRS

Marketing the IRS

Philip M. Leone

gatekeeper press
Columbus, Ohio

Published by Gatekeeper Press
3971 Hoover Rd. Suite 77
Columbus, OH 43123-2839
www.GatekeeperPress.com

ISBN: 9781619848146

Printed in the United States of America

Contents

CHAPTER 1 Is the IRS as Bad as We Think? 1

CHAPTER 2 Can the IRS Be Fixed? 31

CHAPTER 3 A Marketing Approach to Fixing the IRS 59

CHAPTER 4 Risks and Opportunities of this Marketing Fix 79

CHAPTER 5 How to Do It, Part One 93

CHAPTER 6 How to Do It, Part Two 113

CHAPTER 7 How to Do It, Part Three 125

CHAPTER 8 Conclusion—What I Would Do 137

Appendix: My Letter to the IRS 145

CHAPTER

1

Is the IRS as Bad as We Think?

It's a dreary January day in Sacramento, California, and you've arrived at the IRS Taxpayer Assistance Center (TAC) at 4330 Watt Avenue to ask for help in preparing your tax return. Since it's early in the year, you want to get a head start before the tax season gets busier. You've checked the IRS website before leaving home, confirming that the Sacramento TAC doesn't require appointments and is open from 8:30 am through 4:30 pm. When you arrive, you find a line of about fifteen or twenty people waiting outside. Everyone looks a bit confused, and as you walk toward the front of the line to see what's happening, you notice that the doors are locked. There's no sign on the door indicating why the office is closed. It's not a holiday. The others waiting, like you, have come to the IRS for help in either paying their taxes or to get the correct filing forms or for any number of other taxpayer purposes. But, like you, they're waiting outside in the cold, in front of a locked office with no idea why the IRS can't help them on a regular workday.

What happened? I know what happened. I am an IRS employee in the Sacramento Post of Duty and have worked for the IRS for approximately fourteen years. I was there that day and saw people arriving at our locked office. The reason was that the IRS District Commissioner decided to hold an employee "town hall" meeting at TAC, and the office managers locked the doors, essentially forcing all employees to attend. This left no TAC representatives to service the customers the entire afternoon. The Commissioner gave no advanced warning at all—not via the internet, not through a recorded telephone message, and not even from a sign on the door.

You might be surprised by this, but frankly, I'm not. It's an extreme example of poor customer service, but the IRS has earned a well-deserved reputation for horrible customer service over the years. Because I didn't work at TAC, I wasn't invited to the town hall that day, and there were probably enough of us at work to have at least explained the situation to taxpayers if not filled in for the TAC employees attending the meeting. I found out what happened only because my secretary had a bad back that day. I went with her to the first floor to help pick up my department's boxes of mail. On our way to the mailroom, we saw the crowd outside, as well as their obvious agitation. She and I tried to assist some of them by answering several basic questions for a few who, through no fault of their own, arrived for taxpayer assistance from a department that wasn't on duty. For those taxpayers with more complicated questions, we made arrangements for staff to follow up over the next few days. It embarrassed us to face these agitated and frustrated people who had wasted their valuable time coming to the IRS that day. But most of all, importantly, it was unacceptable customer service.

A Horrible Day for You, the Individual Taxpayer

I chose this real-life incident to open this book because it's the kind of perfect storm that happens when terrible customer service and a completely dysfunctional organizational culture meet. TAC had closed without notice so its employees could attend a meeting designed to improve employee morale, or provide some sort of professional training, or some other purpose IRS managers considered worthwhile. However, they neglected to plan for coverage of the office's primary purpose during the town hall meeting: Customer Service. It was a very bad day for everyone—from the taxpayers to IRS employees to the organization's senior managers.

But it's not the only example. Have you ever called the IRS toll-free taxpayer assistance telephone number? If so, you know that it's understaffed, and you've probably waited on hold for a very long time. You can probably draw your own conclusions about the solution to this problem: hire more staff to improve the agency's response to taxpayers asking for help by telephone You might also understand that sometimes government budgets and organizational structures don't allow for this sort of adjustment—one a "normal" business would probably make in a relatively short time. To be fair, the IRS is funded by Congress and, like many other federal agencies, its budget has been reduced. The IRS has also been the subject of certain politicians' irresponsible campaign rhetoric calling for its abolishment, which is certainly not the answer for a government intent on raising its operating revenue.

In other words, IRS leaders and managers down the line in every one of its nine layers of "Government Service" hierarchy of responsibilities are in a tough spot. But they must do something. And when it comes to the problem of long wait times for callers to its toll-free number, what do you think their answer is? It's actually something the IRS calls a "courtesy hang up" or an automatic limit on the time you can wait while waiting for someone to assist you. If no one at the IRS answers your call within this time limit, your call is simply disconnected . . . as a courtesy. Management believes it's better for the agency not to waste too much of your time. You're welcome.

I now work in the IRS Office of Appeals, and used to work in the IRS Small Business Self-Employed Unit. No one wants to be "audited" by the IRS, but anxieties aside, the experience doesn't always need to be terrible. In my case, the process of resolving disputes in the Small Business Self-Employed Unit is classified as an "examination," not an audit, and is generally reported as a positive experience by taxpayers with whom this department of the IRS interacts. These examinations are an opportunity for the IRS to demonstrate good customer service, and, surprisingly, sometimes the agency does precisely that during these examinations. A good examiner—one I like to call a "Goldilocks" auditor because they are not too lenient, not too harsh, understand the tax code, and can communicate with taxpayers—usually resolves issues in a very short amount of time, reaches a verbal agreement, then moves on. It can be the luck of the draw. But later in this book, as I discuss ways to reform the IRS, the positive aspects of the Small Business Self-Employed Unit, and the subsequent Appeals Office that resolves ongoing disputes, may be one place to look for good ideas in improving IRS customer service. Still, even with a Goldilocks auditor, the follow-up period, which is managed according to standard IRS agency protocol, involves a ton of paperwork. Even the best auditor can't help with that problem.

But the "luck of the draw" issue I've identified when it comes to a taxpayer's experience during an audit is very real. That's because, if anything can help you, it's an individual IRS employee. The system itself cannot. In the Appeals Office, both my immediate supervisor and his boss, the Chief of Appeals, had no experience with tax appeals whatsoever. They were promoted based on seniority and therefore incapable of doing the job of the front-line employees and managers they supervised. For this and additional reasons I will explain later in the book, the system needs to be changed if the IRS is ever going to deliver acceptable customer service. Perhaps the reason that stands out the most is that the United States tax code hasn't been substantially updated since 1986—and that's a problem for not only individual taxpayers but for businesses as well.

A Horrible Day for Them, the Corporate Taxpayers

Many of us have heard about the problem of "corporate inversions" in the news. It's the practice of corporations changing their legal home country from the United States to another nation with lower tax rates. Corporate inversions rarely involve the transfer of real executives to new corporate headquarters in new locations overseas. They're strictly paper transactions, completely legal maneuvers resulting in the savings of millions, even billions, of corporate tax dollars. They also represent a corresponding loss of millions or billions of dollars in tax revenue for the United States. There are countries, notably the Cayman Islands, where corporate tax rates are zero or close to it, making them notorious tax havens for corporations that transfer their legal citizenship there. Many articles about these inversions cast the corporations involved as "unpatriotic," and there's no shortage of politicians or members of the press calling for the process to be halted or at least regulated in ways to make it more difficult.

> U.S. corporations already dodge $40 billion a year in income taxes by shifting profits to subsidiaries—often no more than post office boxes—in tax havens. They also hold $2.1 trillion in profits offshore—much of it in tax havens—that have not yet been taxed here. An inversion allows firms to dodge paying taxes on those profits.

> Corporations that renounce their U.S. citizenship and shift their address offshore are deserters. They are traitors to America. They want all the benefits of being an American company without paying their fair share of taxes. That makes the rest of us pick up the tab.
>
> Source: http://www.americansfortaxfairness.org/tax-fairness-briefing-booklet/fact-sheet-corporate-tax-inversions/

Many people are surprised to learn that corporations qualify for tax inversions if foreign shareholders own at least 20% of the company's stock, or if 25% of the company's business is located overseas. This is a low bar, many critics say, and frankly, that's not an unreasonable position. A company that is 79% owned by American citizens, or conducting 74% of its business in the United States, doesn't look like a foreign corporation. But the real problem is a tax code that stands logic on its head in so many ways that this seeming "loophole" is just the tip of the iceberg.

What is the real problem behind corporate tax inversions? Is it greedy corporations who desert our country to escape their responsibility for paying their fair share of taxes? Is it simply closing loopholes for big corporations or tightening the laws to make it more difficult to qualify for a tax inversion? Speaking as an IRS insider, I say there is a different, more effective solution: reform the United States tax code to bring our effective corporate tax rates in line with other western democracies, thereby reducing the incentive for corporations to seek relief from unusually high U.S. tax rates. And there are a number of financial experts who agree with me.

Writing in the April 6, 2016 edition of *Forbes* Magazine, Aparna Mathur observes:

While this may be viewed as a step to "make the system fair," it is time to acknowledge that the U.S. corporate tax system is in many cases patently unfair to its own multinationals and places them at a competitive disadvantage against foreign rival companies that face significantly lower tax bills.

As I have written earlier, the U.S. corporate tax system is out of line when compared to the rest of the world. Not only do we compare poorly when it comes to headline rates, but we are also an outlier when it comes to effective tax rates. Our high tax rates discourage investments and ultimately hurt our own workers. Tax inversions are a symptom of these problems. A tax inversion occurs when a U.S. corporation purchases or merges with a foreign corporation, then subsequently declares the resulting corporation to be domiciled in the foreign country that has a lower corporate tax rate than the U.S.

Source: http://www.forbes.com/sites/aparnamathur/2016/04/06/note-to-treasury-the-problem-is-the-corporate-tax-rate-not-inversions/#34017c115808

In its May 31, 2016 edition, the *Los Angeles Times* reported:

[T]he average tax rate paid by American corporations on foreign income is about 16.7%, according to a survey this year by two Dutch economists. In Ireland, the rate is 5.6% and in Britain only 3.8%. . . . Drug maker Pfizer has proposed the largest corporate tax inversion ever, via a merger with Ireland-based Allergan valued at more than $150 billion. Pfizer has said the combination will cut its effective tax rate to as low as 17% from its declared rate of 25.5%. That's a potential tax savings of more than $1 billion last year alone." That kind of savings is hard for corporate executives to resist, and many of our country's most well-known companies engage in a strategy to recognize profits overseas to avoid high U.S. corporate tax rates. The author if this article makes the logical argument that reforming our country's tax rates to make them more aligned with those of other countries is in fact the way to go. "One hesitates to reward corporate tax shenanigans with lower tax rates, but the logic of restructuring U.S. corporate taxes to match our foreign rivals' has become inescapable. Says Edward Kleinbard, an international expert at the University of Southern California, 'the right solution is worldwide tax consolidation at a fair rate' to shut down corporations' efforts to play one country's tax regime off against another's. The reform might reduce the U.S. corporate rate from 35% to somewhere in the mid-20s, but the result will be a cleaner, fairer, and perhaps even a more productive corporate tax."

Source: http://www.latimes.com/business/hiltzik/la-fi-hiltzik-20151204-column.html

In fact, these same corporate tax rates are a problem for smaller companies as well as huge international corporations. Because our corporate tax rates are among the highest in the world, they affect medium-sized corporations as well as those everyone would agree are really small businesses. When people think "corporate tax rate," they think huge companies like Pfizer or Apple, but small companies are corporations, too. Every year small corporations have to consider turning down business to keep a handle on their effective corporate tax rate because of the significant amount of profits that go to taxes. When I discuss this with friends who are concerned with corporate tax inversions and other techniques businesses use to avoid the high U.S. taxes, I always get the response, “well we don’t mean small businesses.” But small businesses can easily get pushed up into tax brackets that are abusive and not sustainable for owner-operated businesses.

Imagine if not only corporations but every small business and even individual taxpayers in the United States were able to deal with a “cleaner, fairer, and perhaps even a more productive” tax rate? It would take a revolution, you might say, and in a sense, you’d be correct. But this kind of revolution isn’t as sweeping as some might argue. It’s really something that can be accomplished in a series of steps, beginning with the kind of marketing approach international tax experts recommend for fixing our corporate tax policies. And it begins with shifting the focus of the IRS from being completely inward and insulated from the real world to one that looks at the real world and adapts accordingly. That’s not a revolutionary concept, certainly not for a for-profit business, and maybe not even for some government agencies. But what will be revolutionary is making these changes without changing the culture, internal rewards systems, and probably even many of the management practices that now dominate the Internal Revenue Service.

A Horrible Day for Us, the Employees of the IRS

The frustrations individual taxpayers and business executives face when dealing with the IRS are the primary problems that need to be solved, improving the organization. They are a primary reason why I’ve written this book. But another motivation for writing it is to explain why things are so difficult for the people we call our “customers.” And that is to describe the culture within the IRS today and how people who came to the organization with the best of intentions have become discouraged, demotivated, and disillusioned to the point where they are no longer effective at anything other than maintaining their own psychological space while they wait.

What are they waiting for? In some cases, simply the day when they can retire and collect their pensions. In other cases, they're waiting for managers who mistreat them to move on, hoping things will get better when the next manager arrives. Some are waiting to get promoted or reassigned, with the hope of a similar result of getting away from a bad situation in their current position.

And, most unfortunately, there are those waiting for the next chance to vent their frustrations on the people around them—their fellow employees—or worse, on the next taxpayer whose case comes before them for review. To taxpayers, these employees are tax experts. They can be intimidating because they hold the power to interpret and enforce tax policies during audits and reviews; or they can be friendly providers of information and advice for people with questions about how to prepare their annual tax returns.

In a very real sense, taxpayers are right to feel this way. IRS employees know the tax laws, they understand the way returns should be prepared, and they are charged with performing a daily balancing act between fairly explaining and applying our nation's tax laws while firmly enforcing it when necessary. The best IRS employees are what I call "Goldilocks" tax experts. They are neither too harsh nor too lenient in doing their jobs, and they make the best effort to truly understand each taxpayer's situation in assisting them in completing their returns and paying their fair share of taxes. But Goldilocks tax experts are rare. Far more common are the following types of experts—the ones who often make office life excruciating for other employees trying to do the right thing.

We'll begin with the "Expert with an Attitude," an IRS employee who has been on the job for years and is now a short-timer whose heart is no longer in the job. You the taxpayer might have interactions with this type of IRS employee that begin with answers to your questions, or even the employee asking you relevant questions about your situation. But this seemingly helpful and knowledgeable expert quickly fades into a haze of rote answers, or referrals to documents you can read, or things you need to do to help yourself in ways you were hoping the employee could help you. It's important to understand that IRS experts with an attitude *aren't interested in helping you*; they're only interested in making their days as easy as possible by working to the letter of their job descriptions and writing a "clean" report on their interaction with you to justify a positive performance review by their supervisor.

There are many experts with an attitude in the IRS today because a significant number of the agency's employees are nearing retirement age, and they don't want to do anything to rock the boat at this stage of their careers. They've made an assessment of the balance between the benefits of trying to change anything for the better vs. getting along by applying the unique internal rules of their department, or the preferences of their supervisor, or the knowledge they've gained about how to keep making sure they can't be demoted, reassigned, or fired until the day they retire. In any of these cases, they've learned enough survival skills to guarantee that they remain at work until they choose to retire, and in most cases these survival skills have nothing to do with good customer service. They have an attitude because they're at a stage in their careers when they know they're more or less untouchable by their superiors throughout the IRS.

Employees with an attitude might seem like people worthy of disapproval, if not outright scorn. But in some ways, this is unfair to them. They're products of a larger organizational culture that rewards the production of reports that follow a strict format and "look good" doing so rather than taking the risk of honestly discussing real taxpayer issues; they are rewarded for quantity rather than quality by meeting monthly quotas for closing the taxpayer review cases assigned to them; and they are trying to survive in a system that is based on these counter-intuitive job performance measures. Most of them didn't start out this way. They came to the IRS with goals of helping taxpayers and maximizing the tax revenue our government needs to operate. But they probably came up short in the "luck of the draw" that IRS employees face, just as taxpayers face this same element of luck in the experts assigned to their cases. They came up short by spending the formative years of their IRS career under the supervision of a bad manager.

In any industry or organization, employees who enjoy working under the leadership of a good manager can find their careers helped in immeasurable ways; but the opposite is always true with bad managers, and, unfortunately, the IRS has more than its share of these. The result is an expert with an attitude, an IRS employee with low morale and no incentive to do good work; they're just exercising ultimate control over a bad situation by waiting it out until retirement.

The system I envision for improving the IRS doesn't make these employees into the bad guys. Instead, it recognizes their need for job satisfaction and motivation in addition to the small island of control to which they've retreated. It encourages them to find ways to make decisions that respect their own talents and experiences and to apply them to the larger goals of the IRS as a whole. This may include becoming a mentor for younger staff, taking on cases that require the judgment that comes with years of experience, or, in some cases, agreement that it is truly time to retire—that retirement is a time for celebration of work well done instead of the experience of being swept out by the broom of a new management regime.

Another type of IRS employee is the "Expert Who Is Incompetent." Some might say this applies to everyone at the IRS, but as an insider, I can assure you that there is a special category of incompetent people who have been planted and tended to at the agency. They have taken root and are almost impossible to remove. The fact that they contribute to the agency's reputation for terrible customer service is one thing; but their ability to survive, even prosper, in the internal IRS culture and often make work horrible for other employees offers insights into changes needed to improve the organization.

In my years working in the Sacramento office of the IRS, I've seen what is often described as "brain drain." In other words, good employees hired by the IRS become discouraged and beaten down and, after some time, leave for jobs elsewhere. Bad employees tend to stay forever, for at least three important reasons: first, they would find it difficult to get another job; second, they know it; and third, they've learned the survival skills needed to fit into the IRS "system" and outlast anyone and anything that might cause them to leave.

As I mentioned above, the IRS culture is full of protocols that wouldn't make sense anywhere else. Performance evaluation standards are based on a complex ranking system, preference is given for the way reports look instead of what they say, and two meanings of the word "petrified" are used. The first meaning, as in "being afraid," applies to managers who understand the risk of losing head-count in their departments at a time when budget cuts translate these departures into permanent staff reductions. They want to keep people in their department, no matter what their skill level, because once anyone leaves, it's likely no one can replace that employee. The second meaning of petrification, as in "the fossilization of wood and other life forms into immovable stone," applies to the resulting assurance that nothing will ever really change at the IRS—not the tax code, which hasn't been updated since the 1980s; not the structure of an organization that has no incentive to update itself for the twenty-first century; and surely not the job performance of employees who have learned how to write attractive but meaningless reports and score high marks on their annual reviews regardless of the relationship with job performance.

These are the incompetent people you may have encountered in your interactions with the IRS. They follow protocol instead of trying to help, and they hammer the little guy, not because they're mean-spirited or out to get anyone. Far from it. They go after little guys because larger, complex tax returns—such as those filed by businesses with fifty-six different flow-through entities producing inter-related income streams and large investments credited against them—are just too hard to understand. They're incompetent. They go for the simple returns and translate them into good-looking reports and the kind of "clean" resolution of simple issues that scores points on the IRS's performance review system. Unless something changes, these people will be at the IRS until they decide it's finally time to go.

Third are the experts who truly do want to squeeze the taxpayer. Not to be confused with the incompetent experts who choose the easy way out by working on simple tax cases they can process without too much heavy mental lifting, the experts who squeeze taxpayers are people who really have a "gotcha" mentality. They may actually understand the cases of the taxpayers who cross their paths, but they choose not to apply this understanding in a way that helps anyone, allowing a situation they might easily remedy to get worse and punishing the taxpayer for not finding a way to solve the problem on their own. These are the IRS employees who give the agency its bad name; they make bad situations worse and walk away from any responsibility, transferring the blame to the taxpayers. One of them was a colleague of mine who had a customer who made a mistake on his tax forms that both he and I understood caused the taxpayer to substantially overpay his taxes. But my colleague was an expert at squeezing taxpayers and did nothing to help. When I asked him why he didn't bring the mistake to the taxpayer's attention and close the case, his answer was, "it's up to the taxpayer to file an amended return; that's not my job." His answer to the taxpayer who asked for help was, "here's your tax bill."

The interesting thing about the experts who squeeze taxpayers is that many of them treat their fellow IRS employees with the same "gotcha" attitude. They find mistakes in their colleagues' work and report it to their supervisors. They create crises at work that would be humorous if not so destructive. For example, a woman in my department tried to convince our manager that we couldn't brew coffee in the office break room because the smell of coffee made her sick. It's hard to imagine this being taken seriously in any office in the world, but it was true in ours.

I had another co-worker who created an even stranger situation in my workspace. One day as I was using Windex to wipe off my computer, telephone, and file cabinet, a co-worker came running over to my desk telling me that I was trying to kill her. I had no idea what was happening until she explained that she had terrible allergies to chemicals like those in Windex that could damage her health. She demanded that Windex be banned from the office, telling us we had to find other ways to keep our work spaces clean. While a complaint against using spray window cleaner might be slightly less unusual than someone complaining about being averse to the smell of coffee in an office environment, it is still something that wouldn't be taken seriously in most workplaces. More disturbing, this co-worker has since been promoted and is now a top manager, enforcing several of her preferences and quirks as standard office procedure in her department. An example of her managerial behavior happened not long ago when one of her employees left an MBA textbook open at his desk and walked away. Our manager saw the book and decided that this employee must have been doing schoolwork on government time. She called in the employee's previous managers to ask if they had allowed him to study during work time. They didn't know what their fellow manager was talking about, of course, because the employee was a well-respected and diligent worker who never caused any problems. But the manager went directly into making a huge case about the situation, never stopping to think that maybe the employee was using the textbook to look something up for a case he was reviewing. It wasn't as unusual as this manager's early Windex episode, but it was far more destructive because it could have caused serious harm to her employee's career.

Whether or not the tax experts at the IRS fit into the three categories I describe above, the fact remains that there are not enough good employees at the agency. For most businesses, if we were to estimate the mix of employees graded from "A" to "F" in the way we all were ranked on our high school report cards, the spread would look something like this:

Grade A	20%
Grade B	30%
Grade C	30%
Grade D	20%
Grade F	0%

In my experience at the IRS, I would estimate the grades for our employees to fall in a range something like this:

Grades A & B	10% to 20%
Grades C & D	40% to 50%
Grade F	20% to 30%

A Horrible Day for Managers at the IRS: Dealing with Toxic Employees

As we will discuss later in this book, it has become nearly impossible to remove IRS staffers, no matter how much they either fail to do their job or interfere with the ability of their co-workers to do theirs. Two of the most egregious examples of these individuals show just how much bad behavior is actually tolerated.

"Mr. Feet on the Desk." While attending training in my first year with the IRS, a revenue agent in the Oakland, California, office was reading a newspaper with his feet up on his desk. When I asked my classroom instructor and my on-the-job trainers and mentors about it, they told me the following: "Oh, that is so and so. He is angry with his supervisor; therefore, he sits at his desk every morning for several hours or more reading the newspaper and magazines in order to demonstrate his displeasure, his frustration, because he hasn't been promoted, and other grievances." So, he essentially did no work all morning and nobody did anything about it. In front of everybody at his office, or even at training sessions, he sat with his feet up in protest. I had never seen this behavior in any other workplace and could never understand why it was tolerated.

"The Snorer." Another IRS employee, one with the agency

for many years as a secretary/administrative assistant, is an older gentleman who doesn't want to retire. Working well into his seventies, he constantly slept at his desk for long periods of time—and by sleeping, I mean a deep sleep during which he snores loudly enough for everyone else to hear. Employees and managers simply ignore the situation. Some laugh, while others just shake their heads. His direct supervisor tolerates this behavior, setting another example of organizational behavior you're unlikely to see anyplace else.

A Few Real-Life Horrible Days at the Sacramento Post of Duty

Here are three short stories of the real-life frustrations experienced by people who have worked with me at the IRS. There are many more, of course, and I'll introduce some of them throughout the book, because there's nothing like the stories told by those who have tried to do the right thing and gotten into trouble for it, those who have been wronged and been denied any proper satisfaction by the agency, and those who could have contributed a great deal to the organization but became so frustrated that they couldn't stand it anymore and chose to move on to another organization.

Merry Christmas 2015

While the names of all of these individuals have been removed, here's a story from a co-worker, a GS-13, whom I briefly coached in Sacramento. During one of my conversations with him, he discussed how demanding his job was, how it called for skills that were not, in his view, the standard "cookie cutter" approach I believe is too common at the IRS. He complained how upper management showed no appreciation for the flexibility he needed to practice every day. He drew two conclusions that I thought were jarring when I first heard them: "Management does not trust or respect the employees. Management violates taxpayers' rights." When he told me his story, I came to understand why.

He opened a case in November 2015 facing an April 2016 statute of limitations deadline for resolution. He believed there may have been hundreds of thousands of dollars in unreported income, which made the case worth opening even at such a late stage. And, keeping with his responsible and creative approach to his job, this employee arranged with the taxpayer's representative to extend the statute. It was a verbal agreement that would be signed by the end of December, or the case would be closed.

On December 23, just before Christmas break, one of the managers in his territory challenged him about his work on the case. When he explained it, she responded angrily, "That is not a good enough answer. I want that [signed letter of extension] no later than this coming Monday, December 28, or you will close this case by the end of business that day."

My co-worker objected, since this would require him to go back on his agreement with the taxpayer—in other words, violating the taxpayer's rights to carrying through on a verbal agreement. His manager told him she didn't care.

"Merry Christmas," I told him. For no reason at all, except to exert authority, this manager ruined his—and the taxpayer's—Christmas. Because my co-worker had a good working relationship with the taxpayer, he was able to obtain the signed statute extension by the time his manager required it, but that doesn't diminish the larger truth about this incident. It wasn't just bad decision making. It was arrogant, bad decision making.

Being a big thinker, my co-worker saw a larger meaning in this rude exchange.

> We go to town hall meetings where management is supposed to be responding to our concerns, but when we go to these meetings, we have to submit our questions in advance. They just grace us with their presence but don't answer our real questions. They need to be prepped, and they give us canned language as 'answers' to our questions. I don't understand why they can't take the risk of answering tough questions. I would have loved to have been asked about my experience at Christmas time, but I knew that it would never be selected for a prepared answer. When managers choose not to deal with the tough questions, they need to understand that this is seen as a problem by the employees.

Thanks for the Great Customer Service. You're Punished

This next incident happened to me. I've worked at the IRS for a long time, and even though I'm now in management, many taxpayers remember me from previous interactions about their cases, and some of them still call me—or tell their friends and colleagues to call me—because they know I get stuff done. In this particular case, a taxpayer called because he was being billed for taxes he knew he didn't owe and had been trying for several years to resolve the problem. It had become even more stressful for him because he was out of work and was facing financial hardship. I decided to help him and was able to resolve his problem by confirming he didn't owe the taxes for which he was being billed.

My immediate manager and my manager's manager both reprimanded me for my work. They thought I was going over the heads of the people at a lower level of the agency, who were the ones responsible for solving this situation. Of course, from my perspective, they were also the ones that were perpetuating an unjust problem for the taxpayer by not correcting an IRS error. Because I knew the system and understood the taxpayer's situation, I did in fact go over their heads, and the heads of several people at higher levels of the organization, until I found someone who would take the situation seriously enough to resolve it. Oddly, the senior manager I found in this case agreed that there was a problem and fixed it. But he also complained to my manager about me, describing me as a "bull in a china shop." I wasn't following protocol, a problem far more serious in the eyes of IRS management than the concerns of a poor taxpayer trying for several years to resolve an error on our part. Even worse, I was told that if I did something like this again, I would face disciplinary action.

What's interesting about this case is that in fact the department responsible for this taxpayer's problem wasn't mine; it was the collections department. When a senior manager in that department found out about what I did, he sent me a medal of honor for my work. I solved a problem that had been a thorn in their side for the same amount of time it drove the taxpayer crazy. Maybe you've seen another organization where an employee can voluntarily take on the responsibility for solving a customer service problem, solve it, then be both reprimanded by his direct supervisor and praised by the senior manager in the department where the problem had festered for years. I've seen this and much more during my career at the IRS.

I Did the Right Thing. Now I'm Leaving

My final introduction to the horrible days we've all have had at the IRS is a story that isn't exactly about a single day but instead the result of a collection of too many horrible days of an experienced IRS compliance officer. When she and I discussed her opinions about her position with the IRS, she listed four problems she believed needed to be solved yet were not being addressed by managers capable of providing real solutions.

Her first problem was inconsistency among people reviewing the same case, including all factual information and documented interactions with the taxpayers involved. She would often see the same case audited by three different examiners and find three completely different results from each. Worse, she had worked for two different front-line managers during her career at the IRS, each of them very different. There was no consistency in her department's direction from one manager to the next, and she firmly believed these differences weren't based on factual information as much as the personal preferences of each manager.

The second problem she found was a lack of advancement opportunity. She is a hard worker and had taken courses in accounting to the point of being six credits shy of a master's degree. Yet at the IRS she was treated the same as every other employee at her level, regardless of their performance or the skills they brought to the job. In her particular case, as a single mom with two kids, she needed to advance to earn enough money to take care of her family, and she worked hard to accomplish that. But the IRS didn't care. She was still a GS-9 like all the other GS-9s, and she would always be treated and paid the same no matter what she did.

Her third problem was what we call "inventory management" at the IRS, which refers to the number of cases an auditor is expected to close per month. Because that number is high and continues to increase with budget cuts and resulting staff reductions, the IRS rewards individuals who close cases quickly, not those who conduct audits with a higher degree of quality. In this employee's case, she is also someone happy to resolve cases at the lowest level possible—meaning she would help junior employees close them before they ever got to her. This increased her department's overall performance; but because technically these cases never reached her level to be solved, she was evaluated as doing a less effective job than her peers, who would wait for easy cases to solve, taking all the credit.

Fourth, she came to believe that she really wasn't able to help people. Responding to the pressure to use time most efficiently—meaning closing cases quickly and patiently solving problems the IRS believes are best handled by people at lower levels of the organization or by its website and toll-free telephone number—she can't perform work to her own professional standards, even when those standards might be more responsive to the needs of the taxpayers with whom she interacts. Her example of one of these cases was the time a taxpayer contacted her to make a payment on his account, which he owed from an audit that she had conducted. He had at first tried to make these payment arrangements through the toll-free number but was "courtesy disconnected." She decided to process his payment, which certainly solved the taxpayer's problem, but she was reprimanded for doing so by her direct manager. The reason for her reprimand was that helping a taxpayer make payment arrangements is called "disclosure management," and based on a strict interpretation of the rules, this is not a service a professional at her level should perform. Instead, it should be handled by sending the taxpayer to the IRS toll-free number, which of course is where the taxpayer received courtesy disconnects instead of real problem solving. The sad result of these problems is that this employee has since decided to leave the agency, taking with her precisely the kind of commitment to customer service the IRS so desperately needs.

Introducing the Author

Before we go into the next chapters, let me provide some information about who I am and my experience in the IRS. I'm an experienced IRS manager, having worked at the Sacramento, California, office for fourteen years. I have a B.S. in business economics and a master's degree in accounting and have been a licensed CPA since 1994. Professionally, I have worked in a series of investment firms and CPA companies, plus a couple of experiences striking out on my own as an entrepreneur and financial advisor, until I joined the Internal Revenue Service in 2002. Since then, I have been promoted five times and am an Appeals Team Manager, the position I currently hold.

I consider myself to be an unusual personality at the IRS, because I have always been a "go getter" and have taken the initiative to take on challenges, never being one to keep quiet or cause waves. I've prided myself in building teams and intervening in situations requiring the dedicated attention of a skilled and experienced professional, and I believe that this if often the best way to solve the kinds of problems taxpayers encounter with the IRS. And I have learned that this approach to my work has been both a blessing and a curse. It's a blessing because I have never allowed the pressures to passively conform discourage me from bringing my best efforts to my job, every day. It's also a blessing because I'm writing a book about how I believe the organization to which I've dedicated many years can become the agency its mission statement describes:

> To provide America's taxpayers top quality service by helping them understand and meet their tax responsibilities and by applying the tax law with integrity and fairness to all.

The curse has been the difficulties I've encountered with my fellow employees and managers due to my commitment to doing a good job. During the course of my career, I've been reprimanded, written up, sent to anger management programs, and even suspended for "infractions" that, in my opinion, are based on interactions for which I am not primarily responsible. Throughout this book, I'll recount several of these, including times when employees who are "safe" within the system have succeeded in scapegoating me for situations they caused, or others when people resented me for taking initiative and pointed out technical violations of the antiquated IRS "rulebook" that warranted various degrees of punishment instead of praise for my actions.

Have I become frustrated by these interactions? Absolutely. Have I sometimes acted in ways that didn't exhibit the most calm and professional behavior? Yes, I have, and I've paid the price. I've stormed out of meetings I thought were a waste of time. I've criticized trainings and "team building" exercises that avoided real issues or included ridiculous exercises distracting from the problems I thought the agency needed to address. Before moving on with the rest of the book, I want to take an honest look at these aspects of my IRS career. Have some of the consequences of my behavior at work—the reprimands, the anger management classes, even suspensions—been justified? Honestly, admittedly, when it comes to my unprofessional behavior, some reprimands have been deserved, and I regret letting the emotions of the moment get the best of me.

Why Most Days are Horrible Days for Front-Line Managers

Being a front-line manager at the IRS is an awful job, and most, if not all, of the employees working at the IRS know this. This creates a problem because quality employees do not choose to pursue a managerial career at the IRS. The extra pay and potential for advancement are simply not worth it. For example, when someone is promoted to the position of front-line manager, the IRS typically rewards that person with a 10% pay increase. The saying many of my co-workers have for this is "you get 10% more pay for 100% more work and stress." I can't argue with their logic. And therefore, because front-line management is such an undesirable position, the IRS is often forced to promote managers who are not of the highest caliber, because no one really wants the job. The best and the brightest employees at the IRS are smart enough to avoid pursuing a career in management. This is a big problem.

Another big problem for front-line managers is that many who fill these positions pursue them for the wrong reasons. I know fellow managers who pursued these positions because they were nearing the end of their careers and they just wanted to show a higher salary to qualify for a higher monthly retirement check. That's because the federal government bases employees' retirement pay on the highest three years of salary earned during their career. The number of people seeking and receiving promotions during their final years at the IRS is pretty good evidence that employees know how to game the system and also that IRS management allows this to happen. It has very little to do with qualifications or experience. Because I work directly with many of these newly promoted managers, I understand the situation well. Having supervised some of them for years, or knowing their managers, I can say that in many cases they were mediocre at best and did not deserve promotion—not even a merit increase for good performance let alone the added responsibilities that come with a managerial position. But in the upside-down world of the IRS and its staff, these sorts of things happen all the time.

One example is an employee I know who worked at the IRS for about twenty-five years, but this man was not a stellar performer by any means. He often complained about bad management and many awful aspects of the IRS. He was a union steward and had a long history of outbursts against IRS management. He had been passed over many times for a promotion, which greatly upset him, in addition to his union steward frustrations.

Suddenly, as the end of his career began to come into focus, he had a sudden change of heart. He applied for a managerial position when nearing minimum retirement age. And, lo and behold, he was hired as a manager. He confided in me that the only reason he got into management was for the promotional potential. Stuck in the government's structure of employee rankings, he knew that the only way to make any significant additional money was to rise from a GS-13 to a GS-14, and the only way to become a GS-14 was to become a manager. Once hired as a manager, the paperwork began for his promotion to a GS-14 and its higher salary. Because it's the IRS, this paperwork took some time to be processed, but he retired literally the day after his promotion became official, qualifying for higher pay.

Because his office was next to mine, he and I interacted frequently. The day he retired, he told me that he disliked, even hated the idea of being a front-line manager. He sought promotion simply as a way to get back at the IRS and senior managers he didn't like or respect. This wasn't the only thing he did to "mess with the minds" of senior managers throughout his career. He often gave bad advice to fellow employees or led them in the wrong direction—especially the newer ones. He enjoyed giving them grief and playing mind games with them. He told me how much he enjoyed doing this to the point that I believed he had serious personal issues.

He took pride in doing the absolute minimum amount of

work and teased me and other managers for being so dedicated and working so hard. He told us that we were "saps" for not gaming the system, too. Frequently, during management and staff meetings, he would raise issues and objections for no other reason than to disrupt the team from reaching its stated goal and would sometimes wink or smile at me to let me know that he wasn't serious.

He was an extreme example but illustrates those who find their way into front-line management at the IRS. Ironically, managers often discuss how a good manager or supervisor can make or break a new employee. As I've learned too many times in my career, the IRS is more likely to break new employees than make them.

Because I am admittedly a "sap" who has the best interests of the IRS in mind, I complained to my supervisor—the territory manager (who was also this employee's supervisor)—about what he was doing. Our boss didn't intervene against this employee and told me to trust that he was doing something "behind the scenes" to address the problem in his own way. Within a year, however, the territory manager left his position, and nothing was done to address the multiple issues everyone saw as clearly as I did. He got his promotion and retired with the higher pay he managed to arrange for himself despite his disruptive behavior.

Why I've Written This Book

But the question I have to ask—and it is the motivation for writing what I hope will be a book that will help the IRS become successful in its mission—is: *What came first? My behavior, or the dynamics of an organization that should be focused on providing the best possible customer service, while it in fact fails in this challenge and instead allows internal distractions to dominate daily operations?*

Don't get me wrong: I'm sympathetic to the management challenges the IRS faces. Budgets are cut on a constant basis, staff reduction mandates require that retiring personnel are not replaced, and much of the organization's infrastructure—its staff policies and procedures, computer systems, and even the tax code itself—has been allowed to fall into disrepair. Managers, who line staff view as responsible for their frustrations at the agency, are no doubt frustrated themselves. I know I am. But the time has come for us to look for ways to reform the organization, to change it for the better, and to improve not only employee morale but to also focus on making changes that help our primary mission. It's time to create an IRS that is truly dedicated to excellent customer service.

CHAPTER 2

Can the IRS Be Fixed?

As I mentioned in the first chapter, some believe the IRS is so broken that it can never be fixed. Candidates for many elected offices sometimes call for it to be abolished, as if that would solve the problem. Trust me, it won't. Taxes are the cost of living in a civilized society. The IRS mission is to "provide America's taxpayers top quality service by helping them understand and meet their tax responsibilities and by applying the tax law with integrity and fairness to all." It's a mission worthy of defending, and worthy of pursuit. The problem isn't whether or not we need to collect taxes, or whether we need a government agency to perform this function. It's more about how well the IRS achieves its mission, particularly the parts about "top quality service" and "applying the tax law with integrity and fairness to all."

As a long-time employee of the IRS, I want to be both brutally honest in describing the ways the agency fails to meet these two key aspects of its mission statement while remaining sincerely optimistic that the organization's problems can be solved. The story told in this book will detail the IRS's very real failures and outline a plan I believe will bring out the best of what the agency can do to turn its failures into success.

The problems are very real, and there are so many of them that it may seem like there's no way to fix them. Taxpayers may be so frustrated by their experiences with the IRS that they might never want to give the agency a second chance. Some might actually listen to politicians calling for the agency to be abolished. But in fact, the employees of the IRS and its key constituencies—taxpayers, tax preparers, and the public at large—have a number of key things in common.

The IRS wants to provide top-quality service and apply the law with integrity and fairness. Taxpayers, in my fourteen years of experience, generally want to do the right thing (some of my most frustrating moments have involved taxpayers who are simply trying to pay the IRS what they owe, only to find that the IRS makes it more difficult, not easier, to do this). Tax preparers want to get things right. Tax rules and regulations are complicated enough that just about everyone has a question at one time or another, and it's important for the IRS to provide answers in convenient and non-threatening ways. Finally, the public needs the IRS because taxes are an important source of revenue to fund healthcare, social programs, military defense, and other services the government provides. We all have an interest in making the IRS better. Why is it such a difficult goal to achieve?

The answer is that it has become a large organization that has lost its way. Its management structure has been allowed to drift in a way that makes it difficult, if not impossible, to lead staff in a consistent direction. Furthermore, the way employees are supported, trained, evaluated, and rewarded needs a drastic overhaul. Policies and procedures have become outdated, but they are enforced in a rigid and heavy-handed way despite the fact that they clearly no longer work. The management systems in place at the IRS are divorced from the outside world in the sense that they have become games with rules that only insiders can play or even understand. The rewards of winning these games have little or nothing to do with achieving the IRS mission or providing good customer service.

A Categorical Look at the Problems with the IRS

The Internal Revenue Service's mission is to provide American taxpayers with top-quality service by helping them understand and meet their tax responsibilities and enforce tax laws with integrity and fairness to all. We, the IRS, are failing in our mission.

We do not provide the American taxpayer with top-quality service. I would argue that we do the opposite: we provide extremely poor service. We do not help them understand and meet their tax responsibilities. Again, I would argue that we do the opposite.

We do not enforce the tax law with integrity and fairness to all. Once again, we do the opposite. I have broken down why we are failing our mission into three broad categories:

- The tax code and the administration of the tax system
- Resource starvation prevents the IRS from doing its job
- The internal IRS culture, practices, and systems are dysfunctional

1. The tax code and the administration of the tax system

The tax code is overly complex. If you have tried to understand the Internal Revenue Code and its accompanying regulations, you know what I am talking about. You could injure yourself lifting the code and regulations.

The tax code is poorly written. Not only is it difficult to read and understand for the average American, even experts within the IRS have problems understanding and interpreting the tax code.

The tax code is outdated. The tax code has not been revised in a significant way since 1986, when Ronald Reagan was President.

The tax code is biased and unfair. It heavily favors upper-class wealthy taxpayers (the top 1%) over the lower- and middle-class taxpayers (the bottom 99%). The tax code does this by allowing a number of abuses, primarily:

- Corporate inversions, or overseas tax shelters
- Preferential tax treatment for certain types of income, such as capital gains and dividends
- Tax exempt status for interest received from certain investments typically used only by the wealthy, such as municipal bonds
- Favorable deductions for owners of rental real estate (i.e., depreciation expense)
- Special treatment for artificial "flow-through" entities such as partnerships and S-corporations

My experience has been that partnerships and S-corporations are breeding grounds for tax avoidance and evasion. Trying to find the income subject to tax when people earn revenue from these types of entities is like playing the game of "Where's Waldo?"

Wealthy taxpayers hire CPAs and attorneys to protect them. Often, they simply wear down IRS staff because we do not have the resources to keep up with them and cannot possibly take every case to tax courts. I have seen over and over again cases in which wealthy taxpayers pay as much or more in accountant and attorney fees than what they owe in taxes. Lower- and middle-class taxpayers lack the resources to hire this kind of representation and are forced to simply pay what they owe.

2. Resource starvation prevents the IRS from doing its job

IRS computer systems are outdated. I estimate that our technology is twenty years behind current private sector technology. This puts IRS employees and managers at a huge disadvantage in terms of productivity. We are less efficient than what we would be otherwise. I can't imagine how much time is lost because of this.

The IRS is facing severe attrition. The agency has not been able to hire new employees in six years because of budget constraints. The IRS has in effect had a hiring freeze since 2010. In 2002, the year that I joined the IRS, the agency employed approximately 125,000 people. At the time of the writing of this book in 2016, the IRS employs approximately 88,000 people. In other words, the IRS workforce has decreased by 37,000 over the last fourteen years, representing a 30% workforce reduction. But the IRS workload has increased during those fourteen years. Therefore, the IRS is forced to do more work with fewer people.

The IRS has an aging workforce. A considerable percentage of the entire IRS workforce is currently eligible for retirement; 41% of the agency's front-line managers are currently of this age. The problem of attrition at the IRS is an important concern, and it will only get worse in the coming years.

The IRS does not have an effective succession plan in place. This creates what is commonly referred to as "brain drain." The IRS is losing experienced people at a steady pace due to attrition. However, it is unable to replace them with new people because of the hiring freeze. This means that there aren't experienced, qualified people available to train the newer hires.

3. The internal IRS culture, practices, and systems are dysfunctional

The IRS management philosophy is outdated. It is based on a military culture: a top-down mentality in which people are trained to respect the chain of command and follow orders. Employees do not question authority or ask why an order is given, or even if it makes sense—they blindly follow it. The mantra is, "follow that order because you were told to" or "because that is the way that it has always been done." This culture creates "yes" people, which hurts the agency more than helps it.

The IRS has too many procedures. These procedures are cumbersome and constantly changing—a moving target. They are further convoluted, much like the tax code, from individual interpretations based on the understanding of each departmental supervisor. This creates an immense amount of frustration and confusion among employees. There is a common saying at the IRS: "Don't bother to learn the new procedure because it will change again shortly."

There is a high amount of manager turnover at all levels at the IRS. I have had nine different direct supervisors during my IRS career. This constant change of supervisors is disheartening. The inconsistency breeds a lack of continuity, team work, individual work, and overall morale.

The IRS constantly realigns its management structure. The business unit where I have spent many years—the Office of Appeals—has gone through several realignments. Before I left the SBSE-Exam unit, it had also gone through several internal and external realignments. In my opinion, the realignment I experienced first-hand in SBSE-Exam (when the Northern California Area merged into the Western Area) was one of the worst experiences that I have seen in my thirty-plus year career. This particular realignment was handled awfully. The IRS executive in charge of that realignment should have been fired. However, in true IRS form, that particular executive received a promotion. It sounds crazy but is actually quite common at the IRS for people to get promoted for doing a terrible job. The constant realigning of management structures, along with high manager turnover, creates a lot of stress, frustration, and confusion among the front-line employees and managers.

Being a front-line manager at the IRS is an awful job, and the employees know it. As a result, the best and brightest employees generally do not choose management as a career path. Yet the best and brightest employees *should* pursue a career in management in order for an organization to thrive. This does not occur at the IRS because the front-line employees know what a thankless and stressful job being a front-line manager is. The front-line manager job is so bad because, as a front-line manager, you have all of the responsibility without any of the power. You essentially have no authority to hire and fire people. You inherit a team of employees and do the best you can with them. If you inherit a team with incompetent or mediocre employees, you are essentially stuck with those employees. Removing a poorly performing employee once they are past their probationary period is extremely difficult at the IRS. I went through the removal/firing process with one employee and wound up in the hospital for a brief period because the stress was overwhelming. This reminds me of a saying from one of my favorite football coaches, Bill Parcells, who said the following upon resigning from one coaching position: "If you are going to ask me to cook the meal, then you should at least let me shop for the ingredients."

The IRS lacks leadership. Many at the IRS feel helpless. I have heard it described quite frequently as being on a rudderless ship in the middle of the ocean or like being on the Titanic before hitting the iceberg.

The IRS provides horrible customer service to both its internal and external customers. If you have ever tried calling the IRS help line, then you know what I am talking about. It is embarrassing to be part of an organization that provides such poor customer service. The fact that we engage in something called a "courtesy hang-up" says it all. If a private company provided that kind of customer service, it would be out of business quickly. The type of customer service that the IRS provides simply would not be tolerated in the private sector.

Too much internal reporting and documenting is required from employees and managers. No one told me when I joined the IRS that I would be writing so many reports and forms. At the IRS, we make report writing an Olympic event. It's as if we worship internal reports and documents. In the private sector, companies are concerned with making a profit. Therefore, internal report writing by front-line employees and managers is generally not a high priority. In my experience, the IRS internal reports add little or no value to the overall mission of the organization. I can't for the life of me understand why the IRS requires so much internal report writing. A great deal of time is wasted that could be used much more productively. I believe that with fewer reports required—which, as I will discuss later, are structured more to create a pretty picture than to actually document the successful resolution of any issue—everyone at the IRS could be significantly more productive. During my time as a revenue agent, I estimate spending 20% of my time conducting audits. The other 80% of my time was spent on non-essential work (like reports and documentation) not critical to the IRS mission.

There are too many internal meetings and conferences. If report writing is an Olympic event at the IRS, then attending internal meetings and conferences is at least a junior Olympic event. The IRS loves meetings and conferences almost as much as it loves reports. I estimate that front-line managers spend approximately 150 hours per year in meetings and conferences—which equates to almost 10% of their overall time.

Let's recap. In my experience, over 50% of a front-line manager's time is used writing internal reports and attending internal meetings and conferences. Factoring in mandatory training, briefings, continuing education, special projects, and other meetings, I estimate that these take up another 100 to 200 hours per year. Therefore, I believe that somewhere between 50% to 75% of a front-line manager's time is taken up before he or she does anything even resembling what we commonly think of as running a team. This means that 50% to 75% of a front-line manager's time is accounted for before he or she does any of the following: assign work, close cases, conduct informal reviews/discussions, manage the team's workload, take inventory, steer workflow, develop employees' talents and skills, motivate employees, take time for the manager's own self-development, conduct internal/external outreach, meet with taxpayers and their representatives (closing conferences), handle labor relations issues, troubleshoot problems, conduct research, and more.

Is it any wonder why the front-line manager position is not highly sought after within the IRS?

There are too many executives/levels of management. There are seven levels of management between a revenue agent and the top executive in the Small Business/Self-Employed business unit. That is simply too many. It becomes the equivalent of a game of telephone trying to deliver a message from the SBSE-Commissioner (top executive) to the revenue agent (front-line employee). The old saying applies here: "too many cooks spoil the broth."

There is no effective two-way communication. Messages are sent from the top down, not from the bottom up. Honest feedback from front-line employees and front-line managers is discouraged. I will provide an example of this. The IRS Commissioner held a town hall meeting for the front-line managers earlier this year, in March 2016. I attended this meeting and asked a question during the Q&A session. I stated many of the issues and problems that the IRS front-line manager faces. I asked how the front-line manager's job could be made easier by reducing the managerial burden. I stated my question and comments clearly, calmly, and professionally. My comments and questions sparked a good, healthy dialogue. One of the executives on the panel actually said that he agreed with my comments and thanked me for speaking up. The town hall meeting went well, and I was glad I had attended and participated.

Following the completion of the town hall meeting I received many positive comments from fellow front-line managers. I received calls and e-mails over the next few days praising me for speaking up on behalf of the front-line manager and addressing those concerns.

However, not all of the feedback was positive. One senior manager received word about my comments and took them personally. This senior manager contacted my direct supervisor and asked that I be disciplined and reprimanded for insubordinate comments. Luckily, my direct supervisor didn't cave in regarding this request and conducted due diligence on the issue. My direct supervisor made inquiries and discovered that I had in fact done nothing wrong. My not being disciplined or reprimanded really angered this senior manager, who took matters into her own hands and let it be known that I would be banned from her department's work area, or the entire third floor of the Sacramento IRS building. I was very upset over this. I went to the TIGTA office on the first floor to see if in fact I could actually be banned from a portion of the building. The TIGTA officers laughed at this and told me that the idea of me being banned was ridiculous and could not possibly be enforced.

Still, so much for providing honest feedback. I have found during my fourteen years at the IRS that upper management says they welcome or encourage honest feedback, but they really don't. They only welcome positive feedback. They do not want to hear negative feedback or anything that resembles constructive criticism.

The IRS has a "pass the buck" mentality. If report writing and meetings are Olympic events, then passing the buck must be at least a national amateur tournament. Employees and managers at the IRS receive work and often reject it or return it to the sender. It is as if people within the IRS actually derive pleasure from rejecting work and telling their colleagues why they are not required to do the work. The employee or manager will reject the work claiming a form was missing, or that something was completed improperly, or that the most updated form version was not used, or that a procedure wasn't followed properly, and so on. It feels like some employees and managers at the IRS spend more time and effort avoiding work than actually doing their jobs. As a result of this rejection of work—almost all of which travels by paper—we ship an unnecessary number of packages. It feels like we keep UPS, FedEx, and the USPS in business singlehandedly.

There are too many poor- and mediocre-performing employees. There are IRS employees and managers I truly believe would not be able to work in the private sector. These employees and managers have become "governmentalized" from working here and have lost their employment skills or perhaps lacked these skills when hired. We have many employees and managers who would not be tolerated at a private company, especially one that engages in the HR practice of firing employees "at will." Employees can't be fired at will in the IRS. Like I said earlier, it is very difficult to remove poor-performing employees at the IRS. Many of the agency's employees can game the system because of this.

There is a micromanagement mentality at the IRS. I was never micromanaged in the private sector. You either performed or you looked for a new job. I was given assignments and left alone to complete them. Here at the IRS we micromanage people. I do not like to micromanage people, and I in turn do not like to be micromanaged. As part of this commitment I also refuse to micromanage my employees. This often puts me at odds with the senior managers and executives who believe in this micromanagement philosophy. Many senior managers and executives at the IRS are lifetime federal government employees, therefore micromanaging is the only management method they know.

Management is often dishonest. I can't tell you how many times I have had senior managers and fellow front-line mangers state the following: "Wow, I can't believe you told your employees that." The bottom line is that I tell my employees everything. If I know something, then they know it. The idea of keeping information from the front-line employees is something that I really don't understand. I have consistently seen managers at all levels withholding information from employees, telling half-truths, or straight-out lying to their employees. I don't play that game. I am direct and honest with my employees. They know the good and the bad at all times. I believe that people appreciate that about a supervisor. It has served me well, and I have a reputation of being a straight shooter and someone who can be trusted.

Political savvy is an IRS core competency. Managers at all levels are reviewed and graded on how well they perform at political savvy; it's prized at our agency and may be viewed as more important than knowledge and skills. Needless to say, I've always failed in this category. But I know quite a few people who have gone far in the IRS because they are good at politics. I believe that an employee should rise or fall based on their merits, but I've been given the following message by managers at the IRS more than once: "You are smart, talented, and have a lot going for you, but you are never going to get anywhere in this organization because of your lack of political savvy. You ruffle people's feathers, and people don't appreciate that. You speak out too much. Sometimes it is better to just shut your mouth and go along to get along."

Needless to say, at this point in the book it's clear that I've never done that. Life is too short, and no amount of money is more valuable than integrity. To me, political savvy is another way of saying, "Kiss ass and don't make waves." I'm not interested in self-preservation. I'm interested in effecting change in a positive way.

The IRS has unfair promotion practices. Far too often, receiving a promotion in this organization has nothing to do with your competency in the position. This is where political savvy comes into play. Politics has a huge bearing on who receives a promotion, especially at the management level. An employee's annual rating often has no bearing on how well that employee performs his or her job. I have seen employees rated at a 3.4 (an extremely low rating) who excelled at what they do. Conversely, I have seen employees rated at 4.6 or above (a very high rating) who were awful at their job. The annual ratings given in this organization are often not worth the paper they are printed on.

It is far too difficult to remove or demote poor-performing employees. People are not utilized properly in the IRS. I will use myself as an example. I have financial analysis skills and am excellent at motivating people, giving speeches, selling ideas, resolving controversies, and negotiating settlements. However, these skills have not been tapped by senior management. Despite being a front-line manager for over eight years, I have been stuck behind a computer typing meaningless internal reports. I have applied for positions in the organizations for which I am demonstrably qualified but have been turned down every time. People have been promoted to these positions for reasons that have no rhyme or reason to people like myself, who continue to work in jobs for which we are over-qualified. In fact, the annual rating system used by the IRS is itself often ignored in these personnel decisions. Colleagues whom I believe are excellent at their jobs receive low ratings, while people who are borderline incompetent receive ratings of "excellent."

A Few Real-Life Experiences from My Career at the IRS

The problems I've described above may seem academic and impersonal to readers of this book, but for those of us working at the IRS, they translate into very real experiences—sometimes "horrible days," as told in Chapter 1, and sometimes into experiences that last much longer. Here are first-hand experiences selected to illustrate behavior that is not only tolerated but rewarded at the IRS.

Not Thinking Outside the Box: How Many IRS Employees Does it Take to . . . ?

About ten years ago, when I came to work, there was a box on the floor in the middle of the corridor on the third floor of the Sacramento office. A group of about five to seven people stood around the box, discussing the situation, and what they should do with it. For about fifteen or twenty minutes, they talked about how it might have arrived, what might be in it, who they should call to find out what to do with the box, or what forms to fill out. It might seem like fiction, but I assure you this was a very real situation. Eventually, when I walked back through the corridor and not only the box but the same employees were still there, I simply picked up the box and moved it out of the way. Then everyone left, went to their desks, and began their workdays.

It's hard to believe bureaucracies work like this, but they do. Unless you work in one, the way bureaucracies behave is almost impossible to understand. But after my fourteen years in the IRS, I can offer a few insights.

First of all, the unit of reference for staff in a bureaucracy isn't the individual. It's the department. People don't succeed or fail, departments do. When something unexpected happens, like a box in a corridor, it's up to the group to figure out what to do. Responsibility is to be shared, not taken by a single individual. Doing this can threaten the department because people will share responsibility for that individual's action even if they didn't agree it was the right thing to do. Taking responsibility, showing initiative, acting on one's own—these are dangerous things for a group because if one member makes a mistake, all are responsible.

Results are measured by organizational units, whether they are departments, offices, districts, or regions. Individual achievements are lost in this system. There is a high value placed on treating everyone "equally" and in making sure not to single out individual accomplishments or provide negative individual performance reviews at all costs. The result is an organization that rewards "getting along by going along," keeping your head down, and not standing out. It also results in an organizational structure resistant to change and a culture that defends the status quo so strongly that it sees almost any kind of change as a threat. While individual achievements and day-to-day work performance aren't measured in the bureaucracy's evaluation system, individual action that threatens the system is recognized—and punished.

Me moving the box in the corridor solved that morning's problem and allowed everyone to return to work. As it turns out, this was an exception to the IRS rule of punishing individual initiative.

In another situation, I acted in a way that solved a problem but got me into serious trouble. I got a call from a taxpayer needing help with a bill for taxes he didn't owe. No one at the Sacramento office was helping him, he was out of work, and it would be a serious financial hardship for him to have to pay the money the IRS kept billing in error. I took it on myself to look into his problem, asked around the office until I found the right department to help him, and after about four weeks, resolved the issue in his favor. My manager reprimanded me because I didn't follow protocol by going to another department to solve the taxpayer's problem. On the other hand, the manager of the collections department, which had been trying, but failing, to solve the problem, thanked me. And instead of this recognition making things easier for my manager, it led him to reprimand me even more strongly, threatening me with disciplinary action if I violated protocol again.

Eliminating dysfunctional "group think" and replacing it with individual initiative is one of the goals I will discuss later in this book.

Theft Rewarded: Stealing a Computer to Get Revenge

Here's where a few of my personal experiences illustrate the way so many different problems can come together to create such a poor work environment at the IRS. We'll begin with an incident that occurred several years ago. There was an employee who was about as bad as you can imagine a co-worker can be. He didn't do any work and took countless "breaks" while on the job: coffee breaks, smoking breaks, bathroom breaks, you name it, he took a break for it. He harassed his co-workers and went out of his way to be mean. He was nearing retirement but wasn't ready to leave, and nobody in management seemed to want to do anything about him.

He didn't like me at all. I think he was jealous because in the first five years we worked in the same department, I received several promotions. It seems hard to believe, even for me looking back on the situation, but one day he decided to get back at me by stealing my laptop computer while I was away from my desk. I freaked out, and many of my co-workers helped me look for it. Then, magically, after an hour, it reappeared in my mailbox.

Later on, after learning he had stolen it, I confronted him, and we had a heated exchange of words. He was trying to bully me, and I told him, "You're messing with the wrong guy here. I'm not going to put up with this nonsense."

Managers heard our argument, and our union got involved. Our dispute reached the Treasury Inspector General for Tax Administration, or TIGDA, who are basically the IRS's internal affairs office and whose role it is to enforce in-house policies.

After several months, TIGDA came back with their findings: we were both guilty and both reprimanded. I thought their decision was extremely unfair, since this employee had stolen my computer, tried to hide the fact that he was responsible for it, and tried to bully me into dropping my concerns when I confronted him. But management decided to take the easy way out: it was better to reprimand both of us, to not take sides, when clearly there was a villain and a good guy. All I did was raise my voice when he tried to bully me, and management decided we were equally responsible for the incident. It made me feel like I couldn't win no matter what I did on the job.

When this employee finally retired years later, we all believed we had seen the last of him. We were mistaken. One day he came back to the office after retiring, barging his way into his last manager's office and screaming at him, calling him obscene names and creating a dramatic, disruptive scene. It turns out that this manager had been on to him, didn't tolerate his bad behavior, and tried to make him accountable and do his job. This terrible employee's last performance in the office, well after he had retired, was a screaming match resulting in him being removed from the building by security. It confirmed everything we all thought about him—that he was nothing more than a bully and a terrible employee with no interest in doing a good job. Yet somehow, he managed a thirty-year career before retiring. This shows a failure of management as much as it reveals the true nature of this toxic employee.

The Perils of Starting a New Department from Scratch

Another example from my experience of bad management creating problems comes from a 2009 event when I first became a manager. I was given the responsibility of starting a new examination group from scratch, which I expected to be an exciting and rewarding opportunity. Little did I know it would become a painful, never-ending loop of being asked to create a group without any guidance or support, only to find out afterward that senior management didn't approve and wanted me to undo what I had done and start over by doing things their way.

At first, the problems were almost humorous. There was no manual for starting a new group, so my senior manager told me, "It's all on you, Phil. Make it work." That was fine for me. I looked forward to the challenge. Doing everything for the first six to eight weeks was also fine with me. It seemed odd that I had to do everything, from finding real estate space for my new group, to getting cubicles and workspaces and telephones and computers. I didn't even have an office myself; instead I worked out of a conference room and had to take all my papers home every night and bring them back the next morning.

One of my favorite stories was how almost everyone at other IRS locations raised the same objection when I asked for the resources my new department would need. When I called the people who were supposed to help with telephones and computers, or set up a payroll system, they would answer this way: "Okay, can I have your exam group code number, sir?" Of course, because I was setting up a new department, I always answered, "I don't have an exam group code number yet because I'm trying to set things up from scratch, and that's why I'm calling you."

Time and time again, I struggled to get beyond this roadblock. The people on the other end of the line were like robots. Whether you're a taxpayer asking for help or a new manager trying to set up a new department, they can't think outside the box. They follow a script. They don't help. Eventually, I asked to speak with their supervisor, who issued the same request for an exam group number for an exam group that did not yet exist.

I kept going through the same experience with several layers of management until finally someone finally gave me the magic answer: "Oh, you don't have a group yet. Oh, in that case, you need to do such and such." After weeks of this type of work, I had hired my people and had even hired a secretary because I learned the hard way about how many forms and procedures had to be created and followed in order to do my job. I thought my department was ready to go, only to discover that organizational changes from the top would make my job more difficult before it had even started.

Along with this change, we were given a new work plan, with higher goals and objectives. Revenue agents would have to close an average of 3.4 cases per month instead of 3.2. We were going to announce the new work plan at our annual kick-off meeting with employees, revenue agents, and the union. The management team, which now included me, met to think of creative ways to introduce the new plan without upsetting anyone. Amazingly, the consensus position was that we should introduce the new plan but not tell the workers their workload would increase as part of the plan. We planned to leave it to them to discover this "detail" after the meeting so we wouldn't get any push-back from them.

I couldn't believe it and didn't hesitate to stand up in the meeting and tell them.

"I have a suggestion," I said. "Why don't we, as managers, tell the employees the truth? Tell them what's going on, be direct, and be honest with them. Let them know we're in a bind to meet higher productivity and that we need their help; that this is a situation beyond our control, and we're going to need more work from them. I think they would appreciate this more than us trying to sneak it."

Even harder to believe was the reaction of every one of my fellow management team members. They acted like I had three heads, or like I was speaking a different language. Be honest with the employees? Be direct with them? No one agreed with me, and they shut me down. I thought I was trying to be the voice of reason, but instead everyone thought I was proposing insanity. They prevailed. We basically hid the new work plan from our employees, and, along with all the other managers, I had to deal with my team's objections on my own, after the meeting.

But that wasn't all. A few months into my new team's existence, I was told that senior management had decided to schedule a mandatory training workshop for my employees. Two highly experienced managers with long careers at the IRS would teach my employees about the agency at a week-long workshop. I objected, but it didn't matter. The decision had been made by people far senior to me, and we were going to attend the workshop.

As it turns out, it wasn't exactly a workshop at all—it was a stealth evaluation of my employees, and at the end of the workshop, I was told to fire five out of ten of my new hires. Again, I thought this was crazy. I thought my group was pretty good, and although having had to address one or two problems,

I told them there was some good, young talent on my team that could be developed. My managers answered that I didn't know as much as the senior managers running the workshop and to fire half of my new staff before they completed their probationary period. The irony wasn't lost on me at the time about how so many long-term terrible employees couldn't be dynamited out of their jobs yet I was supposed to fire five people after a few months.

Not willing to give up, I pressed for more information about why my employees should be fired. The answers were astounding. They claimed one employee was loud, annoying, and obnoxious and another stupid. They did in fact identify two new hires I thought were problematic, one of which I fired several months later. The other I intended to fire was transferred out of my group and remained with the IRS. As can be expected, that individual remains a problem in the agency to this day. Thanks to my perseverance, I successfully prevented my managers from forcing me to fire the other three employees on their list, and I'm happy to say that they're all doing very well at the IRS today. A few of them have been promoted and are among the more talented people we have.

Gaming the System: Who's Really the Boss?

An illustration of management problems shows how the "petrification" of IRS employees causes some of the agency's problems. It's about a manager with a secretary not doing her job, who wouldn't take direction, and who always caused trouble with other department staff. He wanted to fire her more than anything else in his job, yet he wouldn't. As it turned out, she knew the system well enough to understand exactly why he couldn't fire her. If he did, or if she retired at any time, he wouldn't get another secretary. There was a hiring freeze, and any vacant position stays that way until the next fiscal year, when it simply goes away. She knew she was the last secretary he would ever have and could hold that over him when she didn't want to do too much work. She was wrong about her approach to her job, of course, and her lack of respect for her boss was truly problematic.

Unfortunately, she correctly assessed the way the IRS works. She knew enough to game the system and stay on board. She also knew her boss wasn't about to do his own administrative work, and he certainly didn't want his colleagues to see him doing that after all his years in the agency. She had him just where she wanted him, and she knew that the IRS would allow her to basically call the shots in her relationship with her boss.

If I were her manager, I would have tried to find a way to reassign someone into my department who would become my administrative assistant and then fire her, just to preserve some sense of justice for the organization and dignity for myself. But this was too much for her manager, who sat back and let her run the show.

But when it comes to understanding the problems making fixing the IRS so difficult, don't take my word for it. When I told one of my former employees about this book, he asked if he could help by telling his personal experiences at the agency. He was a great employee with a good head on his shoulders, and I had always hoped he would one day get into management at the IRS. As it turns out, he was too disillusioned by what he saw, and became another example of the "brain drain" making it so difficult for the IRS to improve its managerial staff. Here is his story.

Notes from a Colleague: The Story of an IRS Agent Working in My Department

This final example is from a valued employee in my department who shared his story with me and asked me to include it in this book:

> I started working as an IRS agent in September of 2008. Prior to the IRS, I worked for the California Franchise Tax Board as a Tax Auditor. I left the California Franchise Tax Board for the IRS because I wanted to gain more experience and technical expertise in the field of taxation. In addition, I always thought of IRS agents as intelligent people.
>
> During my first six months as an IRS agent, I went through four weeks of 1040 classroom training. The training disappointed me because it focused more on taking tests than on teaching fundamental concepts of tax law. Thankfully, I made it through since I had worked for a state tax agency, and a CPA firm, and held an Enrolled Agent's license prior to working for the IRS. I noticed during my first year conducting audits that it seemed that the goal of conducting IRS audits was based on closing cases (quantity) rather than quality.
>
> I remember another IRS agent colleague working on a case in which she nearly made a $250,000 tax deficiency. However, since the case was overaged, the agent's Territory Manager wanted her to close the case as a no change rather than keep the case open and close it as an agreed change. As a new agent, I was shocked because I thought that making adjustments to close the "Tax Gap" was more important than closing cases. At this time, the goal for

each agent to close cases was about 3.2 cases per month, which seemed manageable in order to do a quality job.

After my first year, I transferred to another post of duty station. Fortunately, I worked for a manager named Phil, who immediately seemed like he wanted to ensure that his agents did quality and productive work. In addition, Phil wanted to develop his agents to be able to conduct difficult and complex audits and succeed with the IRS. Another thing about Phil, he would 'put his life on the line' for his agents while expecting them to do their work. I was a little shocked by Phil's willingness to do anything to help his agents be successful because I certainly did not get this impression from management in my previous post of duty. The management style and tone at my previous post was the old dictatorship of thirty years ago.

During my four years working for Phil, I developed as an agent by working complex cases and obtained IRS managerial experience by filling in when Phil was out of the office. I have always been a leader for the organizations I had worked for because that is who I am, but I had no interest in working in management for the IRS.

There are several reasons why I did not want to work in IRS management. One reason is because it seems like if you helped and developed your agents, you would be ostracized by your peers. The school of thought seemed to be that managers should treat their agents like slaves rather than employees. Another reason is that the managers seem stuck to their office chair all day, every day, doing administrative paperwork rather going out in the field with their agents. It was not that the managers were unwilling to leave the office, but their office work required twelve to fourteen hours a day.

Case closures were another reason for avoiding IRS management positions. As stated before, when I started with the IRS, the goal was for each agent to close 3.2 cases each month. When I left the IRS in early 2014, that goal had become 4.0 cases per month. The problem I found with focusing on case closures is that it created a Wall Street mentality, where some agents and managers cut corners and sacrificed quality for quantity even if it required unethical behavior. The biggest problem from the pressure to close cases is that not every audited taxpayer was audited fairly in regard to thoroughness. For example, one taxpayer may get an in-depth audit because the agent may not be pressured to close the case, whereas another taxpayer may not get an in-depth audit because of pressure to close the case to meet the monthly closure numbers.

I had hope to make a career and retire with the IRS; however, I could not endure some of the organizational management style that seemed to trickle down from headquarters in Washington D.C. to the local office. I remember agents from my group meeting with our Territory Manager to discuss workplace issues. I left the meeting disappointed due to the fact that the Territory Manager lied to us as if we were toddlers with no life experience. Therefore, I determined that the IRS was about producing brainwashed managers who would brainwash their employees and that no one was allowed to question things or use critical thinking even to improve operational effectiveness.

CHAPTER

3

A Marketing Approach to Fixing the IRS

As discussed in the previous chapter, many IRS problems are based on it being a bureaucracy. Why can't it be more like the private sector? Why does it have to behave in the way we assume is the way all government agencies behave? Why can't it stay on the "cutting edge" of change and innovation to solve problems and become more efficient?

My answer: the IRS needs a total restructuring.

The problems in the agency are so complex and interrelated that any effort to tackle them individually, or without a commitment to organizational change, is destined to fail. There are simply too many people and groups within the agency that band together to stop reform in its tracks. Small-scale efforts to solve particular problems should be implemented—like allocating more resources to install modern computer equipment, developing a human resources system to better monitor employee performance and create a method for moving toxic employees (and managers) out of the agency, or even larger-scale efforts such as restructuring the IRS management hierarchy to streamline its nine levels of seniority into a senior management team better able to communicate and work together. These concepts may succeed in solving the individual problems listed in Chapter 2. But without tackling these problems—or at least the clear majority of them—at once, the organization's inertia and dysfunctional distribution of power to the wrong internal constituencies will almost certainly ensure that the current system will survive efforts to reform it.

Why Incremental Change Won't Work at the IRS

The last chapter of the book lists the problems at the IRS by category along with some examples of behavior I've witnessed. Taken together, they paint a depressing picture of the challenges faced in fixing the IRS. The collection of problems I believe are behind the IRS's terrible customer service are so numerous, and in some cases so entrenched in the organizational culture, it seems they may be impossible to solve.

In some ways, this is a correct conclusion. These problems are impossible to solve if they are approached in an incremental fashion. Improving one department at a time in an office, or one region at a time in the national system, won't do the trick. There are too many problems, too many people at management levels who have no reason to change, and (as we saw) too many employees at lower levels of the organizational chart who have learned to gain power by gaming the system.

Which of these problems would you try to solve first? How long would it take to solve them? What kinds of land mines could current employees and managers throw in the way of progress to thwart any efforts at fixing the IRS? Is there a kernel of a plan for improving the agency that would receive support from a broad consensus of those who work at the IRS?

If these problems and how they appear from inside the IRS seem depressing, well, that's true. It's a very difficult story to tell.

But to create real change, you must understand the real problem. The IRS is plagued by problems resulting from ineffective management, a dysfunctional work environment, the wrong policies and business practices, and resource starvation. Each of these problems is enormous in and of itself. Ironically, because each is so big, change needs to come from a different direction than an effort to tackle each one at a time. Doing that will almost surely fail, because they are so interrelated, and because if three of the problems go unchallenged while one is selected to be solved, the forces behind those other three problems will probably maintain enough momentum for the IRS to continue its dysfunctional ways, causing any efforts to solve that single first problem to fail.

The IRS needs a larger, more revolutionary effort to tackle the entire agency's problems at once. It needs a marketing approach—one which looks for consensus and focus first, rather than slow, incremental gains by solving one problem after another.

At this point in the book, the idea that any kind of change at the IRS can happen may seem impossible. That's intentional on my part. Starting with the next chapter, we'll introduce ways to create real change, starting with a focus on a comprehensive problem that encompasses all four categories of problems outlined in this chapter. Marketing, and the embodiment of good marketing at the IRS—great customer service—will serve as the uniting concept behind all the recommended changes.

It won't be easy; there are many roadblocks, and there are sure to be others we haven't seen that will be equally, if not more challenging. But a comprehensive marketing approach, starting with market research to build a case for learning what IRS customers want, can provide the basis for an outward-facing change strategy, as opposed to one that is aimed at a seemingly endless number of problems that appear if you look inward at the IRS, its petrified management structure, and its obsolete business practices and computer systems. Looking outward will keep change agents focused on the real goal of fixing the IRS. None of the problems I've introduced in the book so far will be solved until the real problem is solved—until we succeed in making great customer service a hallmark of the IRS.

In an organization with fewer systemic problems than the IRS, a management team interested in creating a "turnaround" might consider doing so incrementally. They might look at a series of problems, whether they involve antiquated technology, outdated office procedures, or the need for new staff to replace retiring staff. The team might look at these potential changes and decide to tackle them individually, allowing the organization to absorb them and regain a sense of equilibrium before introducing the next change.

But this won't work at the IRS, in my opinion. There are so many dysfunctional aspects to the organization, and the people who have learned to "succeed" in the system are so intertwined with dysfunctional policies and procedures, the performance measurement systems, and even the work-arounds developed to use antiquated technology to solve today's problems, there is simply no practical way to introduce gradual change. Once new procedures are introduced based on modern business practices, the agency's technology won't be able to keep up with the demands put on it. And then what is to blame? The antiquated technology or a set of new policies and procedures introduced without considering the technology available to be part of any new managerial scheme?

Similarly, replacing people without giving new managers or even line staff the tools they need to succeed, would lead to minimal improvement or even initial drops in efficiency. In an environment resistant to change, the remaining "old guard" could easily make the case that the new system is a failure before it has a chance to make a difference. In any case, if resources aren't aligned behind a new approach to managing the IRS, any effort to make improvements is almost surely destined to fail.

Why A Marketing Approach Can Work

If an incremental approach to changing certain aspects is destined to fail in reforming the IRS, I believe the way to succeed is to take a marketing approach. Meet with the public and ask them what they want from the IRS. The IRS belongs to the entire country, after all. It's a government service, and ought to be responsive to the needs of American citizens. A cutting edge private sector company would do this; they would call it "market research." They might bring in an outside consulting company to create a survey, send it to customers (or, in the case of the IRS, taxpayers), and compile the results to identify key problems and opportunities. These consultants might also conduct focus groups to explore some of these themes in more depth. But their goal would be to understand what customers want, how they feel about the products or services the private sector company delivers, and what they think should change or remain the same for the company to keep them satisfied going forward. Why can't the IRS do something like this?

I wouldn't stop with taxpayers alone. There are other customers for the IRS to consider, including CPAs, tax attorneys, and tax preparation agencies. Finding out what these stakeholders need, what they would like the IRS to be, and how the IRS can work better with the public, would be another valuable part of the market research I propose for the IRS. The public at large should also be considered, in the form of government officials and members of Congress.

Perhaps the most important individuals to include in this market research would be the IRS employees and managers.

External market research results/data would certainly benefit the IRS staff by letting them know what their customers want and need. But asking the employees what they want the IRS to be, and how they see its problems and opportunities, would be a valuable way to engage them in making the changes necessary to create the major restructuring I believe is necessary.

Finding common ground is key. As noted earlier in Chapter 2, we can all agree on the IRS mission and the fact that most taxpayers want to do the right thing. Inviting IRS employees to participate in making the profound changes necessary will accomplish a number of important things: first, it will make the changes less threatening because they will be seen as coming from inside the agency. Even if the changes are based on what taxpayers and other "outsiders" want, creating a plan to implement change from within the agency will respect current employees as they will actually make those changes happen. Making change the responsibility of outsiders coming into the agency to tear it down and rebuild it, isn't much different from abolishing the agency altogether. It's too radical a solution, and it probably wouldn't work.

The other benefits of involving IRS employees include giving these individuals a choice. They can either participate in the changes and go "all in," or they can opt out if they disapprove. Providing an outplacement option for people who want to resign or take early retirement could be a humane way to make changing the IRS more successful.

And finally, for those who want to participate in the change, involving them offers the opportunity for culture change needed to occur as a corollary of the overall restructuring I propose. The "new" IRS would need to stop being a bureaucracy where individuals and their initiatives are less important than the organization and its inertia. Offering individuals at the IRS the chance to contribute their energy and initiative to the process of IRS change would be a great way to send the message that significant change is on the way.

The marketing approach I recommend has three things going for it. First, it addresses a core problem within the IRS: a need for consensus. The problems identified in the previous chapter mostly divide employees from managers, and from each other, no matter where they fall on the organizational chart. There are differences in pay grade; there are differences between people who work in different departments and can't collaborate with each other; there are differences between people who have been at the agency for years and possess vital institutional knowledge, and those who have begun their careers and need to learn from the veterans. In all these cases and more, the divisions among IRS staff members prevent teamwork, individual initiative, and ultimately their ability to provide top-quality service.

The problem of poor customer service is caused by the internal dysfunction at the IRS, such as the misplaced focus on procedures and protocol, and the tendency of defensive people to perceive interpersonal conflicts as a "default" way of relating to other people inside—and outside—the organization. These internal elements of the IRS culture have nothing to do with customer service. And it shows.

This marketing approach to change also addresses the IRS mission in a profound way. Incompetent employees, employees with attitudes, and employees out to get taxpayers don't care enough to do their jobs. In short, they don't take the time to collect taxes in a way that is fair and equitable to all. They take the easy way out. They go after the little guy, avoiding more complicated returns from wealthy individuals and complicated business structures. They shift the responsibility to taxpayers. "It's their job to file an amended return," as one of my colleagues put it when he chose to not help a taxpayer even after identifying a problem which he could have easily alerted that taxpayer about. This should never happen. IRS employees are the experts in our tax system. They should always help others understand and comply with these laws.

So, where does this marketing approach to change begin? In short, it starts with a simple question asked of every internal and external stakeholder: "What do you want from the IRS?"

For taxpayers, of course, that question would be adapted to focus on customer service, including good information, respectful treatment, responsive assistance, etc. For tax preparers, adaptations would be very similar. For IRS employees, the question would be adapted to ask what they want from their job. The common nature of these initial questions will help create a sense of inclusiveness and common purpose. Taxpayers and employees will want very similar things, and they will also root for each other getting what they want as well.

Goals to Achieve in Reforming the IRS

In order to improve the IRS renew focus on its mission, and replace its dysfunctional culture and operations with a new focus on customer service, the process of change itself must achieve its own goals. In short, it must emphasize:

- **Fairness**: People engaged in the change process, both those external to the IRS and those within it, must believe the process is being managed by people truly seeking to do the right thing, and to treat everyone fairly, even those who may disagree with the progress and direction of the change process.
- **Consistency**: The change team must approach its work carefully, developing a plan early, and sticking to that plan throughout the change process. The

consistency of the process will be its own evidence of its fairness, and will be important in maintaining support from the various constituencies involved. Consistency must be maintained in the process itself, as in how decisions are made, how previous decisions are respected as platforms for moving forward, and the involvement and engagement of key individuals and groups. But consistency must also be maintained justifying the continued progress of the change process—the values that drive the change. The importance of maintaining consensus is a key aspect of this consistency. While at times it may be tempting to move forward with a key decision about what change will look like, change managers must be consistent in making sure everyone is on board with where the process *is*, not where it is going. A willingness to move more slowly than some may prefer to bring everyone along is a key element of what I call "consistency of the process."

- **Customer Approach**. The point of reforming the IRS is to benefit its customers—United States taxpayers. Remembering that no improvement is worth making unless it advances the agency's ability to better serve its customers will be a key filter in reviewing and evaluating ideas.
- **Caring and Compassion**. The managers of the IRS change process must be strong enough to maintain progress toward the design and implementation of a successful plan for reforming the agency, yet they must remain aware of the need to respect and empathize with the needs of others. People

like myself, who have battled with many fellow employees and managers over the years and have been burned attempting to reform the agency from within, might not be good candidates for this job. We might be too harsh in our judgment, and create problems by seeking justice instead of improvements. The idea that it would be better to have "too many winners" in order to succeed is part of this commitment to caring and compassion. So is a willingness to support individuals with training or generous retirement and outplacement services when the time comes for these inevitable decisions.

- **"Goldilocks"**. In the first chapter, I talked about the high respect I have for IRS examiners, auditors, appeals managers, and others who have internalized the values of being not too lenient and not too harsh. These same values will be vital for those in charge of the reform process.

An Overview of the Change Process

Having introduced many of the problems at the IRS that can only be seen from an insider's perspective, and having hinted at some of the characteristics of the change process I propose, we're at a transition point in this book. We're moving from a look at the problems—the reasons *why* we need to change the IRS—to considering the requirements I believe are necessary to succeed in changing—a look at *how* we will change the IRS.

As I stated previously, there are larger principles involved in creating successful change. And, like many similar broad principles in other planning initiatives, they contain specific elements that can be adapted in the face of new developments, or better information, to keep things moving forward. But the four key principles themselves will always need to be maintained. Here is a short overview of the process, organized by those four principles. Much of the next four chapters of this book will involve the details behind these principles.

Building a Strong Commitment to Change

An important first principle because in an organization like the IRS—a large, old agency filled with people whose self-interests might motivate them to resist change—creating a consensus around the need to change is a vital first step. The ways I believe are best to build this consensus are by first asking questions, kicking off the process with a carefully-designed research process that invites participation as much as it looks for answers, and one that assures people that participating will not lead to negative consequences. These are difficult considerations to balance; after all, it's likely some people will be found to be in the wrong positions in the agency for effective change, and anyone suspicious of being on this kind of "list" will need assurances of fairness and transparency from day one. There will also need to be assurances that any possible negative consequences will be mitigated as much as possible. In other words, whether it's through the promise of generous severance agreements or early retirement arrangements, leaders of the change process I propose will need to ensure that there are as many winners as possible—even among those who might rightfully fear they might be among those who will lose.

The research process - first actual work of my change process - won't be the beginning of that process, however. The real beginning will be a higher-level plan to introduce the process in its entirety, with an emphasis on broad principles, a deliberate and fair approach, and a commitment to transparency and thorough communication. The first announcement that a change process is coming will produce a range of responses, many of them emotional. Some will welcome the idea of a fresh start; others will fear losing their jobs; still others will yawn and cynically ask, "what else is new?" Leaders must be ready for all these potential responses, because all will certainly happen.

This kickoff announcement will serve several purposes: it will discuss the need for changes in the agency; it will talk about the process in terms of how it will be conducted, including major milestones and an overall timetable; and it will introduce the research phase and its associated questions that will actually begin the work. Finally, like all other phases of my proposal, it will invite participation and feedback from all involved, both those inside the IRS and stakeholders from outside, such as individual and business taxpayers, government officials, the press, etc.

Finding a Solution that will Actually Work in Bringing About Change

The first practical step in our change process is to find a solution that will work. This process will take time because a comprehensive solution will be difficult to discover and articulate. It will also take time because of the need to convince everyone involved that the solution will work, and that the process of arriving at this solution has been fair, inclusive, transparent, and considerate of all stakeholders' interests. This step is important, because while it may be possible to avoid specifics in the initial announcement that change is coming, that same opportunity won't be as available in this first step. Finding a solution means designing a research process to gather information necessary to drive the rest of the change process, and it means doing so while preserving consensus, commitment to participation by all, confidence that a positive outcome is possible, and, above all, a willingness to provide honest and thoughtful information from those invited to participate in the project's research.

The research phase also includes more than simply designing a questionnaire and taking it to groups of inside and outside stakeholders; it also means creating a "change team" to serve as a kind of board of directors to guide the change process through this and all subsequent phases of the work. Making sure this team is itself inclusive of all stakeholders, and that it functions in a way that is representative and transparent, will be a key element in this first action phase as well.

Selecting the change team will include balancing not only the representative quality, but also the number of people on the team. The temptation will be to create a large team, in order to assure key stakeholder groups that their interests are represented. But the larger a committee becomes, the harder it is to function. Finding the balance between representation and size is a familiar challenge to this sort of initiative, and there will be precedents in other large organizations that can be explored to find a workable strategy at the IRS. But assembling this change team will still need to be done with a full understanding of the groups within the IRS and from its outside stakeholders to ensure gathering good information, and also that key constituents will be satisfied that the research phase is a fair and comprehensive look at the issues to consider in reforming the agency.

Maintaining a Broad Consensus of Support Throughout the Change Process

This is perhaps the most difficult challenge to be faced in reforming the IRS. Once specific issues are identified, there will be immediate concerns among people involved in the process—and from those observing from outside the change team—that the research phase hasn't gotten to the core problems behind the agency's current situation. Maintaining a focus on getting the right answers is a technical measure of quality that will exist regardless of the outside opinions, or dissenters within. Compromising this quality cannot be considered a good answer in managing a successful change process, particularly at this early stage. But defending the fact that the right research questions were selected, the right people were asked, and that their answers were assembled and analyzed in the correctly will be the work of the change team and its leadership. Part of the answer will be to hire a skilled research team—whether a "market research" organization, or led by an academic institution, or some other professional research team is assembled will be decided by the "board of directors" IRS change team. But once that team has begun its work, and throughout the research phase, up to and including issuance of a final report, the job of providing it with the managerial required to complete its work will be up to the change team.

As noted earlier, maintaining consensus means moving slowly and emphasizing communication and transparency as much as results. The danger of getting things wrong is one thing, but the danger of having the right answers shot down by excluded people or those improperly engaged in the process would be far more regrettable. Setting expectations of quality, inclusion, and transparency as key elements of the change process, and delivering on them, will be the job of the IRS change committee throughout the process I'm outlining. They will have the right to make adjustments and change direction when necessary; but they can never waver in their commitment to the core principles behind changes in tactics.

Following Through with Resources, Patience, and Respect

Transparency and inclusion cannot be achieved through communication alone; they eventually need to be supported with actions seen as responsive to stakeholder concerns throughout the change process. Making decisions based on thoughtful consideration of options, announcing the decisions and the reasons, then carrying out the initiatives and hard work required to achieve the goals behind these decisions, are as much a part of a transparent process as anything.

There is always the risk, of course, that these actions will be challenged or resisted. In fact, these sorts of roadblocks will certainly happen during the process I propose. What is important for the IRS change team is to be sure that there are always enough resources to carry out its plans; that it always acts with the patience required to achieve objective results while maintaining a broad consensus of support; and that its actions are conducted with demonstrable respect for all stakeholders involved. There is no guarantee that a program as ambitious as a sweeping IRS change will succeed. There will be a number of events and problems outside the control of the change team no matter how thorough it performs. |But failure will almost surely result if the change team abandons its commitment to any of the factors it can control.

"Too Many Winners": One Problem We May Have to Live With

Again, there is no incremental way to change the IRS for the better. But this doesn't mean that a deliberate, gradual methodology cannot be used to plan these changes. In fact, as I will argue later in this book, that is probably the only way to change the IRS. A slow process of committing to change, assessing where change is needed most, building consensus around these needs, and following up with a similarly deliberate effort to design a change process not only likely to succeed but that also supported among all stakeholders is what I recommend. It may be maddeningly slow, but the organization's "business as usual" has become so insular, so divorced from the realities of what would be considered usual anywhere else, that tackling it will require building strong commitment to change, clear analysis of necessary changes, and a nearly bullet-proof plan for implementing required changes. Consensus will be needed among all stakeholders—both outside the IRS and within.

Everyone—even people who can't stand Windex or coffee aroma in their workplaces—will need to see the benefits of these changes. Nobody—or at least as few people as possible—should faulted for the current system *even if they clearly are.* Failure to realize this important aspect of managing the change process will only lead to resistance, and with so many people responsible for the current system, it might be easy for one group of individuals who feel unfairly blamed for the system's failures to seek support from old guard members to build a large team opposing change. There will be costs unacceptable to people without the experience or perspective on the cause of the IRS's current situation. There will be people who might seem to be rewarded when they "ought" to be punished.

The fact remains that with so many people inside the agency invested in the current system, changing it will require their cooperation. Some people might think, "oh, the heck with it, let's just fight the good fight and eventually prevail. The system is already so bad, who cares if it's disrupted. How much worse can it become?" I understand this point of view and in fact have my own scars to prove that I've tried this approach. My perspective, which has grown over many years, is that things can get worse. They might never change. Trying to reform, or improve, or reorganize the IRS and failing *is* worse than leaving things the way they are. Abolishing the IRS—the call of some politicians who rely on simplistic slogans to win elections—is also worse, because in my opinion there are no simple answers to collecting tax revenues in an increasingly complex, international economy.

The current system might outlive many people who begin the slow change process I'm recommending. But it won't outlive all of us if we remain dedicated to the principles of (1) building a strong commitment to change; (2) finding a solution that will succeed in bringing that change; (3) maintaining a broad consensus of support among stakeholders throughout the implementation of the change process; and (4) following through with the resources, patience, and respect for everyone involved along the way. The change process I recommend is summarized in these four primary commitments. The specifics of the actual change process I propose may not be the best, and I'll accept a better idea develops. Success is important, and success in a task as complicated as reforming the IRS will require a strong team of committed people who believe in the process, and trust each other. More people may "win" as a result of these changes than might be objectively fair. But if we don't change the IRS for the better, all of us stand to lose, and lose a great deal more. For the record, after years of losing struggles within an organization I desperately want to change, I want to win. And if winning means sharing with too many other winners instead of getting even with people whom I think deserve to lose, so be it. Let's share the benefits of a new and better IRS broadly. Let's start figuring out how to create it together.

A Brief Look at the Remaining Chapters

Now that we've explored some of the reasons why the IRS needs to be reformed, and my optimism about the possibility that the agency becoming a successful, customer-service-driven revenue generation system for the federal government, it's time to take a look at how I've organized my proposal for making this happen. The next chapters describe the change process, and are organized as follows:

- **Chapter 4: The Risks and Opportunities of This Marketing Approach**

  This chapter looks at some of the reasons behind my optimism, along with the dangers lurking for anyone trying to take on this admittedly huge and risky project.

- **Chapter 5: How to Do It, Part One**

  This first of four chapters about the change process start at the beginning: recruiting and creating a change team involving all key constituencies, and how this team begins fact-finding work while maintaining an early and consistent focus on maintaining consensus.

- **Chapter 6: How to Do It, Part Two**

  This second step in the change process involves gathering results of the change team's fact-finding activities, and preparing the IRS internal culture for the changes to come.

- **Chapter 7: How to Do It, Part Three**

  This third step outlines how to bring the changes approved in steps 1 and 2 to the IRS. It focuses on the successful implementation of an internal change plan, creating a new customer-service oriented culture and readying the IRS for its new and improved operations. The final step in the change process brings the services of a reformed Internal Revenue Service to the taxpayers, or customers. It is the culmination of everything that has gone before it, and its implementation is a sign that the agency—along with its employees—is truly ready for its new role.

- **Chapter 8: Conclusion—What I Would Do**

  The book will close with some of the personal reflections from writing this book, including a look back at a long career and a hopeful view of the agency's future.

* * *

The process of changing the IRS is not without its risks. In the next chapter, we will look at several of these risks. Leaders of the change process will need to reinforce and maintain the "we're all in this together" belief. They'll need to convince all stakeholders that the process will be objective and fair, and give people options for the degree to which they want to participate in the changes coming to the IRS. Transparency, frequent communication, a degree of flexibility, and most of all patience will be required for the proposed big changes to become reality. The marketing approach described in future chapters is a classic model for creating significant organizational change: start with research involving basic questions; make sure changes are based on well-understood and accepted answers to these questions; and create a meaningful dialogue with those participating in the entire change process.

CHAPTER

4

Risks and Opportunities of this Marketing Fix

CHANGING AN ORGANIZATION with one of the worst reputations in the country into one of the best records of customer service is an enormous challenge. Even your state's local Department of Motor Vehicles is probably more highly regarded than the IRS—a sad, but deserved reputation. It's also a sad fact that two barriers to change include the likelihood of substantial resistance from within the organization, and reluctance by opportunistic politicians to give up the benefits of having the IRS as a punching bag to rally voters with claims that they are going to abolish the agency or drastically simplify it beyond practicality.

The People Risk: Changing a Culture Filled with People Resistant to Change

The ultimate vision of change can be threatening, particularly to long-time employees of an organization committed to undergoing major change. Employees and managers may fear for their jobs, and in some cases, this is warranted. Even people who remain may find their power reduced, or find these changes to be too foreign to be comfort. They may need to learn new job policies and procedures. Protocols that once provided a safe haven for a predictable, nonthreatening work environment may be eliminated. New skills may need to be learned and practiced. Evaluation procedures that could be easily navigated to produce long-term job security, even rewards, might change so drastically they can no longer be the foundation they have always been.

The way a dysfunctional organization can provide safety and power for people who know how to "game" the system can be remarkable—until you see it first-hand. For example, in many IRS offices such as Sacramento, budget cuts result in a strategy for reduction in force relying on waiting for employees to leave on their own volition, then simply not replace them. There's no strategic design for a smaller, leaner work force There are no incentives, such as outplacement or early retirement, for people whose departure might be best for organizational efficiency. There's simply a waiting game. People who retire or resign, take their jobs with them when they go. It's a heck of a system. But it gets worse. People in secretarial positions can use this lack of strategy in force reduction to their advantage. If they leave, their executive supervisors won't get another secretary. When a secretary reaches retirement age and can live comfortably on a pension, the normal power relationship between an executive and secretary reverses. The executive must please the secretary or else the secretary can leave and the executive will be without support. Even worse, the executive will need to type letters, take phone calls, and do various tasks which make the job look less managerial and more menial. It's actually a funny thing to witness, particularly when the executive has it coming. But it's still a heck of a way to run an organization.

Beyond the risks brought to the process by the behavior of individuals within the IRS, there is also the weight of years of momentum, or inertia, throughout larger departments, offices, and regions that form part of the agency's bureaucratic identity. Old timers have survived countless battles with bad supervisors, training initiatives, reassignments to other regions, or even past reorganizations. They've probably done so by finding ways to wait things out, quietly resisting change by doing the minimum necessary before changes turned out to be the fads common in an organization adept at maintaining the status quo.

Sometimes this sort of passive sabotage can be more willful and deliberate, especially when a particular organizational unit comes together to resist change. Because an organization is full of old-time employees and hasn't seen major revisions of its policies and procedures in more than three decades. doesn't mean it is ripe for change. On the contrary, there are probably powerful forces within that organization that make change difficult.

The ways in which an agency like the IRS resists change can actually be impressive. Sometimes units that move together to keep the status quo can look like icebergs, or tectonic plates, that shift on a scale seemingly too large to comprehend as an intentional response to a threat. What do I mean by this? A few years ago, the California District used to be the California Region, on a par with the Western Region and other large IRS units. We had clout, and were also very good at doing our job. We were consistently one of the leading regions in achieving or exceeding our goals—so good that we became a threat to other regions unable to match our performance. Our reward was an involuntary merger into the Western Region, consistently one of the poorer-performing regions, masterminded by other IRS regions tired of us making them look bad. Our new, larger

Western Region became one of the mid-range performing regions once our strong performance combined with the rest of our new region's poor performance. We became "average" for no other reason than the other regions wanting to look relatively strong in a new world of equals.

A business that allows this sort of organizational restructuring to happen for no legitimate business purpose is, as stated above, both ripe for change and ready to fight that change tooth and nail. The regions that knew how to use the system to their advantage and redefine the California Region will surely feel like they can probably outlast any new change efforts, while employees in California might view new efforts to change the IRS with cynicism, given what the last organizational change did to them, and why.

The Policy Risk: The Challenges Inherent in Updating 30-Year-Old Regulations

As mentioned earlier, The Internal Revenue Code and regulations that accompany it are outdated They haven't been revised since 1986. They are also convoluted and poorly written. Experts cannot decipher the code, let alone the average taxpayer. The code needs to be simplified, since it is thousands of pages of confusion. It is so unreadable that in different cases, it produces several different answers depending on who you ask. It is also loaded with special interests/lobbying efforts. It is unfair. In general, the tax code favors the top 1 percent of the American taxpayers, not the vast majority you would think are its primary focus given the IRS mission statement. We need everyone to pay their fair share of taxes. It is unfair to rest of us when someone—usually the richest and most powerful, who can afford lobbyists and lawyers —skirt their tax responsibilities. Here are a few examples:

- **Homeowners receive favorable tax treatment in comparison to renters.** The home owner may deduct mortgage interest payments and property tax payments, but renters can't deduct anything in relation to their residence. This is sometimes justified as a way to make home ownership easier to achieve, because the "American dream" is to own our own homes. But it is a policy that deserves to be reviewed in light of the way wealthy individuals use real estate as tax shelters, or how landlords are unfairly given advantageous treatment over their tenants. Some states, such as Massachusetts, allow residents to deduct a portion of their rental payments from their taxable income. It's not a foreign concept to help a majority of Americans who work hard and pay taxes but cannot yet afford their own home.
- **Owners of rental real estate are allowed to deduct all expenses associated with those properties, including a depreciation expense.** Depreciation expense makes sense for depreciable assets, such as vehicles, office equipment, office furniture, and machinery. These assets truly decrease in value over time and only have a certain useful life. However, real estate historically increases in value over time, making it an appreciable asset. Claiming depreciation expense on an asset that *increases* in value seems counterintuitive, yet the tax code allows it. In a sense, it is a form of double-dipping, because the owner makes money on the appreciating value, while also getting a tax deduction. This is classic case of having your cake and eating it too.

- **Passive activity losses are allowed to the extent of non-passive income.** However, there is an exception to the rule for rental real estate: Passive losses from rental activity are generally allowed up to $25,000, but real estate professionals are not subject to this $25,000 limit. The real estate industry clearly has a powerful lobby interest in Washington, so large property owners continue to receive this type of extremely favorable treatment.
- **All income is not created equal.** W2 wage earners are taxed at ordinary rates, which are the highest rates in the code. However, if a taxpayer receives income from capital gains and/or dividends, they will be taxed at a much lower rate.

In summary, the tax code is slanted towards the wealthy top 1 percent because they primarily receive income from rental real estate, stocks, and bonds. Therefore, they receive favorable tax treatment over the remaining 99 percent who primarily receive our income from W2 wages, taxed at the highest rates. Warren Buffet, one the richest people in the world, has stated that our current tax system is unfair. Specifically, his secretary pays a lower percentage of income tax than he does. Therefore proportionately, the secretary has a higher tax burden then Warren Buffet. This is clearly a gross injustice—one glaring enough for a beneficiary like Warren Buffet to point it out.

A Bad Combination: Outdated Regulations and a Dysfunctional Culture

The IRS internal organization has problems that, in my opinion, are directly related to the outdated tax code. It's worth reviewing one last time before looking at ways to reform how the agency values substance over form, and rewards a "check the box" tunnel vision management that does little to address problems of efficiency, time management, cost-benefit analysis, fairness, or customer service.

Like the tax code itself, the IRS culture is outdated and unfair. It's like the entire agency, along with the tax code, is stuck in the 1970s and 1980s. It still operates under old rules and systems. For example: imagine working for Google or any cutting-edge Silicon Valley high tech company. Now imagine working at the IRS. Talk about night and day. I recently read that Google employees are given 30 percent of their time to do whatever they want. Could you imagine that in the IRS? IRS employees have to account for every minute of their time in such detail, they probably spend 30% of their time filling out reports accounting for their time. It's clearly a case of form over function, reporting over performance, paperwork over productivity.

I worked for 20 years before joining the IRS. Not one previous job required me to document or track my time to the degree required by the IRS. The IRS requires employees to document and record a tremendous amount of information. Not only must employees track every minute of their time, they must explain just about everything that they did during that time. The amount of documenting and reporting that IRS employees and managers are required to do is illogical. It often feels like the job is more about filling out internal reports and checking boxes than the job itself. The IRS values reports, not people. Can you imagine how much more efficient the IRS would be if we did not require so much internal reporting? Can you imagine this as part of a reformed IRS?

I was a Revenue Agent in the Small Business and Self-Employed division from 2002 thru 2009. In this position, I would go out into the field conduct audits. I would arrive at a business at 9 a.m., where I would meet with the taxpayer(s) and/

or their representative(s). I would conduct an initial interview, review the books and records, make an audit determination, and issue the audit report. Ideally, all of this would happen in one day. The taxpayer and/or representative would sign the report and pay any tax liability in full. However, I would then have to spend the next 3 business days typing up a report and organizing the written file.

How effective is this process? In my opinion, this is highly wasteful. We should only need to document a case file in great detail if it is an unresolved audit and could possibly go to Appeals and/or tax court. If the taxpayer is happy and the bill is paid in full, why are we spending so much time producing detailed reports for the IRS's internal records? During my time as a Revenue Agent I estimate spending only 10 to 20 percent of my time performing actual audits. The rest of my time, I was reporting. I estimate closing approximately 300 audit cases in 7 years as a Revenue Agent. I can only imagine how many more cases I could have closed without the burdensome internal reporting requirements for cases that truly did not need it. Because I am a numbers person, I estimate I could have conducted *twice* as many audits, or 600, without these constraints.

Where to Start: Imagining Change When the Need is Overwhelming

Most people begin their plan for changing an organization in a way similar to creating a "to do" list. They list the changes they believe are necessary, and review them—first, to make sure nothing is left out and that there are no duplicate tasks; and second, to prioritize. It's my argument that, when it comes to changing something as large and dysfunctional as the IRS, creating a priority order this early in the process is a mistake.

Because there are so many places where needing change, and because so many people will legitimately fear they are part of the problem and not the solution, a priority list may quickly be seen as a "hit list" of organizational elements and individuals eliminated for the organization to become successful. And, of course, the idea that someone is under attack is the surest way to guarantee opposition. Reforming the IRS will always be a tricky process, and approaching it will always require sensitivity. This is especially true as the process begins.

Unless the change process begins by defining itself as a *process* with no pre-conceived notions about where change will lead, it will probably fail, and fail early. To an outsider looking at the change process I recommend, it might appear to be a process without any goals. Avoiding a prioritized "to do" list might even remind some people within the IRS of the ridiculous training programs we experienced, with coloring books, group singing exercises, and other "team building" activities. But in fact, the process I recommend has a very important goal, one that must be maintained at all times. That goal is consensus.

Without a broad initial buy-in and continuing support, the temptation to feel threatened. and therefore, mount a counter-attack. will be too much for anyone feeling left out to resist. Over time, this consensus will become a strong foundation for creating change, and make difficult decisions more likely to succeed because they will be understood as the result of a fair and caring process. The entire process will surely appear unacceptably slow for those seeking results, and for those thinking there are so many obvious problems that it's best to start somewhere, and to start now.

But in my experience, the organization has become so divorced from the realities of successful organizations that building a new foundation to support future change is absolutely necessary. The shift to difficult decisions and decisive action will come, but will come slowly and deliberately. Managed correctly, this slow and deliberate process stands the best chance of success.

Building consensus doesn't mean that everybody watches and evaluates the change team, giving or withholding support based on their own priorities. I It means that everybody does the work, and everybody enjoys the rewards. Those are the two important pillars on which my process's consistent commitment to consensus rests. People will be active in building and maintaining consensus, because they will be involved. They will participate in deciding what facts are needed for the change process to succeed, and how to fairly and accurately gather those facts—.

Therein lies the trick to making the change process successful. Instead of exploring and evaluating the necessary changes, and in what order, the change process I recommend begins with a look at how the process will proceed as its first step. This removes a great deal of fertile ground for disagreements, arguments, and blame, replacing it with a more neutral and supportable agenda as a path to success.

There will be more about this in the next chapter, but think about it briefly in the context of the organization I've described. If you were a manager in the process of gaming the IRS system, would you want to be part of a change process beginning with a search for things needing reform, followed by decisions on which needed to change first? My guess is you wouldn't, and you might, like several of the colleagues I've introduced, do all you can to disrupt the process and deflect attention any problem involving you. Multiply that by a few hundred or even thousand, and you have a recipe for a process that stalls before it begins.

Even those who don't have their own agenda will be skeptical, to put it mildly, that any effort to change the IRS will succeed.

A process starting with neutral fact-finding and efforts to build a consensus-driven plan is also the best way to overcome objections from this constituency—a constituency, by the way, including people within and outside the IRS. The IRS has a deservedly terrible reputation. Some of it has been earned by the people in charge, or employees who have long ago given up on making real contributions or achieving real job satisfaction. But some of the problems at the IRS are caused by resource starvation and the resulting reliance on antiquated equipment, policies, and procedures. Other problems are the result of wealthy taxpaying individuals and corporations who can afford lobbyists to carve out loopholes, exemptions, and other special treatment at the expense of others. These outside groups may be the most difficult to engage in the change process, or to even prevent from trying to sabotage it from the beginning.

In short, it's going to be tough. But if you're going to do something analogous to threading a needle, you have to make sure you're aiming the thread in the right direction. That's precisely the idea behind two key components of my plan. First, we'll need to begin the process with an open mind—with an approach emphasizing dispassionate fact-finding and consensus as its two most basic and consistent values. Second, we'll need to focus on customer service above all—including a sense of either internal justice that rewards and punishes IRS staff, or external justice that rewards and punishes different groups of taxpayers. It's an approach with the best chance of preventing an onslaught of self-interested attacks from multiple groups, and also the best way to create enough intellectual and political space for identifying key problems and defining them in a way that will maximize their support- and therefore the plan's overall chance for success. Again, ultimately there may be "too many winners" and a feeling that ultimate justice has not been served in all cases. But if the IRS becomes a truly customer-driven organization operating on a consistent standard of efficiency and a "Goldilocks" approach to matters within its own span of operations, this plan will be an unqualified success.

A Practical Perspective: Keeping an Eye on Consensus, Communication, and Mission

Creating a change team large enough to represent all constituencies, yet small enough to get things done, is a key step to be discussed in future chapters. For now, we're still talking about leadership, which can be provided and articulated by a select few individuals at the top of the IRS organizational chart, plus a possible few Congress members or the private sector (such as a Warren Buffett or Bill Gates type of reform-minded benefactor).

This small core leadership group will provide the foundation for future activities of the change team, establishing a focus on the IRS mission, a dispassionate fact-finding approach to the change process, and an operational style emphasizing transparency and open communication. Members of this core leadership will need to be able connect the IRS mission to the primary goal of changing the agency. This can be our marketing approach of emphasizing customer service, but leaders can also keep the door open for another primary goal identified during the fact-finding.

Leadership, and later the representative change team, will need to emphasize consensus, one initially focused on the overall plan for an objective and thorough fact-finding phase. Later, as the fact-finding phase shows results, the team's challenge will be adapting their strategy for maintaining consensus to include the results of the fact-finding. The change team will face this challenge over and over again as each phase of the project produces results and replaces broad goals of "change" and "customer service" with more specific goals such as, "revising the tax code," or "supporting taxpayer management of online interactivity with the IRS."

In each case, the change team will need to work on creating a new, higher consensus level with each finding or recommendation, while ensuring consensus is achieved before proceeding to another round of findings and recommendations. This will involve not only a thorough explanation for why each finding and recommendation deserves support, but also a reminder of the original goals of the change process, and why these new concepts are consistent with that original vision. I It also means involving everyone, even if this means creating different strategies for gaining support from different constituencies.

The change team will almost surely need to rely on "surge protectors" at times, including timetable flexibility for completing an individual phase of the process, but no flexibility on achieving the plan's ultimate objectives. Another surge protector might be needed to solve difficult consensus-related problems, such as offering early retirement IRS employees who need to change, but can't or won't. The change team will need to be willing to learn along the way, and not become overly dogmatic or rigid. After all, being rigid and dogmatic are key reasons the IRS has problems in the first place. Constituents who go above and beyond their change goals—in this case, mostly IRS employees and managers, although some taxpayers and tax preparers might qualify—need to be rewarded for their efforts. While the formal plan calls for all internal changes to be in place before the plan is brought to the taxpayers, it may be necessary to include previews of the benefits of coming changes to these external constituencies.

Above all, the change team must maintain a realistic perspective. The challenge of reforming the IRS is a big one, and may not succeed. But the marketing, customer service-focused program recommended here is the best approach we have, and deserves our best efforts. The alternatives, such as abolishing the IRS, are unsustainable and unrealistic. And, to mention the one factor providing optimism that real change is possible, there are many good people within the IRS who will welcome the chance to reform the agency and make it a true customer service organization.

CHAPTER

5

How to Do It, Part One

THIS IS THE first of four chapters offering practical advice managing the restructuring of the IRS. Given the risks of an organization that seems perfectly adapted to resist any kind of change, it's going to be quite an adventure.

Buckle your seat belts. Let's go.

Step One: Form a "Change Team" from Within the IRS

The first recommended step is an organization-wide effort to form a "change team" inclusive enough to represent all major internal stakeholder groups. Each of the nine layers of management would need to be represented, as would all the national regions, and the major functional departments: collections, audit, and all others. The reasons for this broad representation are twofold: first, it gives the effort a fighting chance by allowing for input and participation by all major groups within the agency. Second, it provides a defensive line against possible mischief or outright sabotage by organizational units that might want to resist. The "change team" would function more as a board of directors or policy-making body, than as an active staff department or management team. This is also intentional and accomplishes a couple of things.

First, it keeps the team focused on big issues, which will be key to preventing fragmentation into smaller, rival groups that might form around particular initiatives. Second, it recognizes that the first phase of the change effort itself involves market research—a skill that no one at the IRS currently has. The new IRS change team would in effect hire the consultants to carry out the assignment of designing the questions to be asked among IRS staff, and ultimately taxpayers and tax preparers. These consultants would, with the change team's approval, conduct the research, compile the results, and report back findings to the change team. The change team would be responsible for identifying the changes the research found most important to the IRS internal and external stakeholders, and organizing them into a change process structured into early, middle, and late-stage phases.

Think Phases, Not Priorities

Note that I'm proposing phases rather than priorities, an important distinction because priorities single out some problems as more important than others, and, by extension, single out some people as more to blame for dysfunction than others. While this will almost certainly be true, starting a major—and risky—change process with even the hint of an unequal distribution of blame may create more problems than it solves. Organizing problems into phases allows the schedule to rule more than the problems, and gives the change team opportunity to group problems into phases based on the need to keep the organization unified through the process.

For example, each phase can include problems that touch all regions, all managerial levels, and all functional departments. This may seem counter-intuitive if one or two problems are at the core of the IRS's most serious failures, but sometimes the most strategic approach is one that recognizes the organization's current culture while envisioning the one we want to create.

Once the market research is completed and its results are used to create an approved change plan including multiple phases, the responsibility for managing the change process would need to be assumed by IRS senior management. This may or may not require a change in senior management before the process begins, and perhaps this decision ought to be made at a higher level. A national commitment to this change, with a Presidential appointment and Congressional approval for a new IRS Commissioner, might be necessary to keep the process from losing momentum before it even begins. But, because this is something that's out of control, the plan assumes that the IRS itself is committed to making these changes, and that there is no need to appoint a new Commissioner to make it happen.

Step Two: The Change Team Also Needs External Representatives

The external people joining the collaborative change team I propose will include three key stakeholder groups: taxpayers, tax professionals, and policy makers. Within each group, we need to make sure those who make up the team are representative, collaborative, and committed to the recommended change approach. While at first glance this might seem easier than assembling a team with similar characteristics from those inside the IRS, external members may not be easier to select, or be more likely to stay on course throughout the change process.

Let's begin with the taxpayers themselves. There are wealthy, middle class, and lower income people. There are those who file as families and as individuals. There are young people concerned about whether there will be social security when they retire, and who may not fully understand the differences between the types of taxes withheld from their paychecks. At the other extreme, there are retirement age people collecting social security and enrolled in Medicare. The interests of each type of taxpayer are different, and if each advocated for their own self-interests, there would be chaos, to say the least.

And those are just "individual" taxpayers. There is also a similar range of business taxpayers, from individual proprietors through partnerships and various types of corporations—LLCs, Chapter Cs, small businesses, large multi-national corporations, and nonprofit organizations. They, too, have self-interests, and if they were only interested in tax reform "better" for them than what we now have, it's highly unlikely that we would be able to rely on them to collaborate on bringing real change to the IRS.

These reasons further underscore the need for the change team to be not only representative, but focused on broad issues designed to unite, not divide, people from so many different perspectives.

Tax professionals might be a blessing in the external member organization of our proposed IRS change team. Because they see all different types of taxpayers each year and help them prepare taxes, they are perhaps the group with the broadest real experience of taxpayer and IRS interaction. They might be useful allies in keeping others focused on the broad customer service issues that will form the early consensus-based plans for bringing change to the IRS.

Policy makers, on the other hand, will probably be the most dangerous members of the change team, with the possible exception of certain IRS management who might make their way onto the change team. I'll include elected officials, as it takes little imagination to realize that a seat on the IRS change team could be a powerful asset for someone seeking election to a higher office. Academic institutions, the press, and nonprofit organizations committed to fair tax policies would need some sort of representation, even if they are less likely to want to use their participation in the change team for their own personal advancement.

Essentially, this short look at the external people to consider for change team membership shows that the team might be large enough to be unwieldy. Also, a risk exists that any one of the selected members might find it hard to resist the temptation to come to the process with pre-formed ideas about the best specifics of any new tax policies and/or tax rates that would ultimately be included in the results of the changes.

The keys to managing this risk are two-fold. First, as noted earlier, the early tasks of the change team are to design and conduct market research among internal and external stakeholders about the changes needed to improve the IRS. Designing this initial research, and making sure it asks for information to define broad, sweeping, consensus-oriented themes for change—ideally centered around customer service and the broadest possible concepts for development of a "fair" tax code—will be the only task for the change team at this first stage.

Second, as the list of interest groups included in the external change team might get big enough to form a committee too large to do any real work as a whole, organizers of the change team will need to find ways to break this single large committee into a network of working groups, each of which is charged with a specific sub-task related to the change team's overall mission.

This will be tricky as well. With different types of individual and business taxpayers recruited to the change team, it might be tempting to form subcommittees related to their specific interests. For example, recruiting a subcommittee focused on small business concerns might make sense, as might another subcommittee comprised of low-income taxpayers with families.

This would be a serious mistake, since it would create reasons for the larger committee to segment into specific sub-groups, each of which with its own idea of what a successful IRS fix might be, and the likelihood that conflict would develop among these groups based on self-interests. Instead, the larger change team should be segmented into subcommittees based on interests that cut across taxpayer distinctions. That is why my emphasis on the first phase of bringing change to the IRS emphasizes ways to improve customer service. Everybody wants better customer service—both those inside and outside the organization. Keeping this as the change team's first order of business is perhaps the best way to maintain consensus among all team members.

Step Three: Professional Staff Who Provide Needed Expertise to the Change Team

Marketing professionals experienced in the development of market research will certainly be part of the change process, although they will most likely be hired consultants, rather than members of the change team. The team, in all its broad, possibly unwieldy representation of individual and business taxpayers, plus tax professionals and policy makers, will work with the marketing professionals by directing development of research methods and tools to create the questions about reforming the IRS that will (a) begin the process of change in a constructive way, and (b) make sure the research is based on broad, consensus-building conceptual change rather than specific, detailed changes.

In addition to the marketing professionals developing the research tool, there will be other professionals whose involvement will be critical to the long-term success of the change process. These include professionals to advise the change team and marketers, such as organizational behavior experts, strategic planners, and financial experts, along with public relations professionals who only observe the process during its first stages but will later play an important role in communicating the changes that will signal different stages. Their expertise in developing future messages about the rollout of our plans to fix the IRS will include not only the message itself, but the way in which that message is rolled out, in order to maximize positive responses, or even interest and anticipation.

Whether the team is structured into a few or many subcommittees focused on specialized themes related to the overall challenge of fixing the agency, it also requires different roles from the IRS members vs. external representatives of taxpayers, tax professionals, and policy makers. Essentially, there will be an "actors" vs. "advisors" division of members, with the actors comprised mostly of IRS employees, and the advisors being mostly external representatives.

Step Four: Who's on the Team?

The internal IRS stakeholders on the change team will need to be carefully selected. As mentioned at the conclusion of the last chapter, people like myself won't be good candidates - we're too close to the problems, and we have well-developed ideas of who should be rewarded, and who should be punished as the IRS is changed and reformed. So, the first qualification for joining the change team is impartiality, and a willingness to manage an "open book" of possible problems to be identified as important enough to be solved as the agency transforms into a customer service organization. This may seem obvious given the content of this book to this point, but making sure we look at who not to include on the change team is worth reviewing one final time before discussing who should be "drafted," if you will, for team membership.

Internal team members should be drawn from the ranks of employees and management—again, something that might seem obvious to non-IRS. But remember, there are nine layers of management at the agency, and including one person from each layer would require a relatively large change team—even before considering people to include from outside the agency. My recommendation is to think of the different layers of IRS professionals in terms of broad layers, avoiding the use of the federal government's standard division of labor. In other words, think "front line employees," "junior, or front-line managers," and "senior managers." These three categories can keep things broad enough to select internal change team members to represent the agency without picking one from each GS (or government service) layer, resulting in nine internal representatives.

This makes sense from two perspectives: first, it keeps the change team small enough to get work done in the process. Remember, consensus is the most important goal of the early change process. The larger the team, the harder it will be to achieve and maintain the precious harmony and agreement necessary to move forward. Second, if looking at reforming the IRS, a team charged with changing it shouldn't start by re-creating the current organization structure. Nine layers of management might or might not make sense, but a change team mirroring the current hierarchy might be inadvertently biased toward keeping the status quo during planning. That would be a mistake. Fewer and smaller is better than larger and more representative.

Emphasizing a small change team is important because, in the interest of creating a broadly representative team, there will be pressure to expand the team. Compromising in order to balance the efficiency of a well-structured change team vs. the need to represent key constituencies will be an unavoidable agenda item in this first phase of the change process.

Remembering the fact that it's better to have too many winners than too few, the change team may need to be larger than initially planned. That sort of compromise is good at this early stage It is far more important to maintain consensus than to be seen as being rigid and dogmatic about something as abstract as the size of the change team. Big and unwieldy is problematic, but in the grand scheme of things, a big and unwieldy team that works together is less of a problem than a lean and efficient team lacking the support it needs to perform because it is seen as unrepresentative of people whose cooperation will be critical for successful change.

External change team members will include the broad categories of taxpayers, accountants, and policy makers—three critically important but potentially large groups. Taxpayers will include individuals, businesses, and nonprofit organizations, since even these organizations pay their share of taxes. Creating other categories needing representation, such as finding representatives from political not-for-profits, associations, foundations, and cause-oriented community organizations should be resisted, since there is potentially no end to the number of different groups that can be "qualified" for membership on the change team due to their unique organizational characteristics. Put another way, it's true that a community health center has a different operational model than a trade association, even though both are nonprofit organizations, broadly defined. Similarly, a hospital differs from a private physician practice group, which both have for-profit and not-for-profit versions. Representing all would guarantee a change team so large it would not function efficiently.

The same considerations would also apply to businesses. It might seem logical to include a manufacturing corporation and a service company on the team, as well as individual proprietorships, partnerships, and corporations. But we can't include every type of business by products, services, organizational structure. C Difficult choices will need to be made. The saving grace in making final decisions about which groups are represented and which are not, will be the fact that the change team's mission to conduct a fact-finding program, not making decisions on its own. Like the different GS levels of the IRS, different types of taxpayers—businesses, individuals, nonprofits, etc.—will either be represented on the change team, or the change team will include them developing a research plan to accurately capture their interests and goals from the outset.

From my perspective, there is no right or wrong way to structure the team, other than broad parameters like those mentioned. It must be representative. It must be small enough to operate efficiently. It must be composed of individuals committed to the delicate balance of maintaining consensus and achieving successful change. And it must be transparent in communicating its work and thinking to vast numbers of interested outside parties whose support will be vital for the team to do its job well.

How this works in practice is something for the change team itself—and its leaders—to achieve once the grand adventure of reforming the IRS begins. Whether it happens next year or many years from now, it will happen in a world different today. Those differences may be small, or they may be great, but will be real enough to require that my recommendations be broad enough to support specifics that only future change agents will know. The people selected for membership in the change team will need to have credentials that most constituencies—internal and external to the IRS—agree are impeccable, or at least good enough to attract and hold together a high level of consensus and support. Those who choose this team will in many ways determine the success or failure of the process as it takes its first steps. I wish them all the best.

Step Five: Creating a Research Tool

In my opinion, the best way to launch the change team as an active leadership structure is to charge it with researching the problems that must be addressed in making the IRS a successful customer service organization. The credentials mentioned above for change team membership will need to include not only respected knowledge of the IRS and how it operates, but will also need to carry over to the development of a research tool that is impartial, on target, and qualified for use as a list of IRS changes.

More importantly, they will need input from research participants to credibly represent the ideas of outsiders about what needs to be changed. In short, there will need to be a professional market research component to the change process, one from an outside firm hired by the change team.

The first action of the change team is to review candidates for the assignment of designing and administering a research tool to capture input from taxpayers with standing in recommending problems to be solved. Note that I said, "problems to be solved," not "changes to be made," or anything implying a solution at this stage. Remember when I said the process would sometimes be agonizingly slow? This is an important example of why that is necessary. The change team's first job is to create a consensus foundation as changes are considered, accepted, and planned later on. That consensus will also need to withstand the most difficult of all phases—the actual implementation of those changes–with the requisite people who will be unhappy with changes going against their own perceived interests.

That means the change team will need a lot of consensus, and will be putting much foundational support "in the bank" in this first. Taking things one at a time means developing a research tool—a questionnaire, in all likelihood— to gather information about perceived IRS problems, and work for all constituencies, inside and outside the IRS. To accomplish this, the questionnaire will need to be adapted to meet the needs IRS employees and managers, along with different types of taxpayers and other external constituencies. But it will also require structural consistency so that the questionnaire results can be collated into a standardized set of identified problems for review and acceptance by all. The market research management requires sophistication and experience of professionals, which is why I believe the change team must hire the best possible consultants to manage this important part of the change process.

Another type of professional organization that critical to the earliest step will be a marketing communications firm. No doubt many individuals and organizations will resist change from day one: employees inside the IRS nearing retirement are one possible group; wealthy real estate owners likely will not want to lose the advantages they and their lobbyists have gained from the IRS.

A good marketing firm won't need to single out these possible "objectors" and develop strategies to blunt their possible opposition. Instead, this consultant organization will serve the change process more effectively by creating a broad consensus for impartiality and fairness of the research. This positive message—one that emphasizes the change team's desire to get things right, to be fair and compassionate, yet firm and effective—is more likely to succeed than a portfolio of individual strategies designed to address and overcome a laundry list of possible objections from different groups resistant to change. Again, this is a skill that will almost certainly be beyond the professional skills of the change team itself, requiring it to vet and hire an outstanding communications representative.

Step Six: What Does the Change Team Actually Do?

I knew you were going to ask this question, and it's a good one. The change team's primary job is to represent all key constituencies, and to build and create consensus as it manages the overall change process. It will need to engage professionals with specialized skills, such as market research and communications (a.k.a., public relations). These professionals will be tasked with designing research tools and conducting communications programs that produce results: accurate information about solvable problems, and a dialogue with constituencies ensuring they are truly represented in the process of identifying problems and maintaining the good will necessary to solve them. These are, as I said, results, and they are the responsibility of professionals hired by the change committee. The committee itself will focus on its own important job: maintaining a fair and successful change process.

The change team will need to set, and meet, a list of expectations and values defining the process from the beginning, and maintaining these expectations and values as its work continues. First, the expectations, which I believe can be listed as simple bullet points:

- The process will be fair.
- The process will be inclusive.
- The process will be transparent.

- The process will lead to real change
- The process will achieve results for
    - Taxpayers
    - IRS employees
    - Government policy makers

The change team will also need to maintain a consistent set of values, differing slightly for each phase of the change process. For this first phase, those values will include:

- **Consensus**: everyone involved will be given the opportunity to be heard, and be invited to support the process regardless of its ultimate outcome. This value will be consistent throughout the change process.
- **Credentials**: members of the change team will be qualified to manage the change process and be seen as qualified by all participants and observers, both inside and outside the IRS.
- **Representation**: the change team will represent key constituencies, either directly, or through the design of a research tool and communications program capturing the input, interests and ideas of everyone.
- **Impartiality**: the change team will be demonstrably fair and willing to consider the interests and ideas of all constituencies without pre-conceived bias.
- **Compromise**: the change team will be flexible and willing to adjust its planning and operations in order to consider the interests of groups whose continued engagement is critical to the success of the change

process. Such compromise will be real, but it will never deter the change team from its overall mission of impartially and efficiently identifying problems, evaluating them, selecting problems to address, and effectively solving them.

- **Facts**: all activity in this first phase will be directed at finding demonstrably true facts through research and an ongoing dialogue with all constituents.
- **Transparency**: everything the change team does will be communicated openly to all constituents, and all communication will include the opportunity for dialogue with people who wish to voice views and ideas.
- **Communication**: open, honest, frank, and timely communication will also be one of the values consistent through all phases of the change process.

A head-start on solvable problems (author's perspective)

In describing the process, I believe will bring the structural changes required at the IRS, I can't resist providing a few of my own answers to the question of what problems need to be solved. If the change team asked to provide this input, my answers would include the highlights below.

There's simply too much paperwork. Taxpayers will probably agree with me on this one, particularly those involved in an audit. The sheer number of reporting forms is a characteristic of the work that has gotten completely out of control. But the situation is far worse for those of us at the IRS. Not only do we process all the forms we require from taxpayers, we have our own mountains of paperwork required to document everything we do. The long list of steps in our work process end—and sometimes begin—with internal forms required as evidence of our work, ready for the next employee to do his or her work. We document everything, and I mean everything. Paperwork is still a literal problem, because we work in the language of printed papers and file cabinets. Even if we digitized our process, the requirement that we document everything would still be a problem. Mountains of paper are a symbol of the wasteful and time-consuming procedures the IRS requires. The main issue is that it's time to streamline the way we work. Saving millions of trees along the way would be a very nice benefit.

There are too many controls on IRS employees. Remember the earlier stories about being reprimanded for solving problems by going outside of the narrow restrictions of department and not making any waves? The consequences of this problem aren't only the low morale these restrictions create, or the stifling of individual initiative and even the early departure of good people who can no longer handle the frustrations of being boxed in. They also result is poor work produced by people stuck inside the system.

An emphasis on the group—the department, the office, the region—has the ironic effect of making that group less productive. When teamwork is discouraged, even in the name of "teamwork," a group of professionals ceases to provide the level of quality work they could otherwise deliver with updated or removed IRS protocols. The incentives the IRS protocols provide to employees are the ones described in earlier chapters: "keep your head down, don't voice your opinion even when asked, and be a good boy or girl." The problem of too many controls at the IRS is actually related to the tons of paperwork in many ways. When the lengthy list of strictly enforced internal procedures is pared down essentials, we'll save not only trees, but people too.

The way these incentives have gradually stopped the IRS from evaluating its work based on real success, and replaced a focus on the mission of "applying the tax law with integrity and fairness to all," to one that emphasizes the production of attractive reports.

We have replaced our mission with methods as the primary goal of what we do every day. This is partly the result of years of gradual increases in the protocols IRS managers enforce at the agency. Another part of it is the consequence of a bureaucracy turning its attention away from individuals, to groups as the primary unit of measure in work evaluations. There is also a kind of "race to the middle" in terms of organizing the agency so that high-performing units and low-performing units are combined to create new parts of the organizations whose measured performance fits more closely with established averages in other units.

A symptom of the way the IRS performance evaluation has changed for the worse can be found in the vague and impersonal language permeating every page of these evaluations. We can't single out people, and we can't say anything that might offend anyone or make them feel isolated from the group. The result is a feeling that we're all inside of a big box in the middle of an even bigger box, and that it's useless to try to escape. Instead, we survive by following procedures in very visible ways, and expressing individuality in quiet victories, like helping individual taxpayers and hoping we don't get reprimanded, or in moving boxes out of the hallway instead of being part of a group that wonders whether that's really a good idea.

The tax code needs to be updated. Thirty years is long enough to wait for this to happen. Reagan was President the last time there were substantial changes. There was no e-mail, no internet, the Soviet Union was still intact, and we went home from our work to watch television shows like "Cheers," "Murder She Wrote," and "Miami Vice." Speaking of work, employees at large organizations deciding to use computers were given "workstations" connected to a central processing unit (CPU) that received everything "keystroked" in, then distributed that information back to us and to every other workstation in the system. The real world has changed in dramatic ways. It's time for our tax code to catch up. Sure, we've added new pages to the tax code and increased the number of forms to complete and procedures to follow. But the fundamental way our tax system works is still mired in a world nobody under the age of 40 remembers.

* * *

The problems I re-introduce at the end of this chapter are a reminder of what real change will mean to the IRS. The detail problems—dysfunctional management, too much paperwork, toxic employees, a thirty-year-old tax code—are as formidable in scale as they are in number. While it's worth reminding ourselves of the details of the IRS's problems, it's important to frame them more as parts of a whole than as individual incremental challenges, celebrating a series of small victories on the way to a final triumph that achieved by solving a final problem.

I do not recommend that approach. This chapter provides a glimpse of how a marketing-based approach can help fix the IRS. It introduces the key internal and external stakeholder groups that will need to organize and come together to begin the change process, and the additional "change agents" who will help them move forward to create the research tools and procedures to identify the goals for unified change. That process—starting with a process that identifies large but not necessarily detailed goals for change—is an important first step, because it is an agreement that change is necessary, possible, and broadly defined for everyone to buy into and continue to work towards. Getting too specific introduces the risk of the change team splintering into factions believing one type of more detailed change is more important than another, or that the process of change needs to proceed in a specific way different than what others might think is best.

It might seem counter-intuitive, if not counter-productive, to begin a process leading to so many large-scale changes to avoid specifics when the change process begins. But in my opinion, that's the only way of discussing specifics in a way that will be more than an academic debate but that's where we are. Remember, this is the first of four chapters focused on how to fix the IRS, each of which describes one of the four phases of the change process I describe. It's the first step, no more than that, but certainly no less.

CHAPTER

6

How to Do It, Part Two

THE FIRST PHASE of the work I've proposed to transform the IRS is the development and execution of a market research program asking key constituents what they want the IRS to be, and to identify the key problems they think need to be fixed to become successful in its mission. Once the marketing consultants selected for this assignment draft their questions and run them by the change committee, there will be a systematic question and answer period of at least several months. When a sufficient number of internal and external stakeholders have weighed in with their answers, it will be time for the second phase of the process: writing and issuing a fact-finding report to summarize the results of completed market research, and outlining proposed changes, organized by future, inclusive phases instead of priorities.

Step One: A Fact-Finding Report

As noted previously, this is when the change committee transitions from a "board of directors" presiding over the work of professional marketing consultants and communications professionals, to a leadership team supporting IRS senior management in creating and maintaining consensus throughout the organization as change begins. But this second phase is still one of transition. The change committee will still work with the marketing and communications consultants to review research results and organize them into a coherent list of targets for change forming a foundation for success. These changes need to be described concisely to be understood by everyone inside and outside the IRS. They need to be organized in a way that supports action - there can't be lengthy debate about whether to move the box out of the hallway at this stage. The message of this fact-finding report must be that the correct targets for change have been identified, that solving these problems is not only desirable but achievable, and that everybody can be involved in making the changes necessary to successfully transform the IRS. It's a critically important phase requiring work by marketing and public relations professionals, combined with IRS senior management, and the support of every member of the change committee.

The fact-finding report resulting from this phase will be, in a very real sense, the mother of all paperwork ever produced at the IRS. It will be the blueprint for an organizational revolution. Every possible kind of threat to its success will arise at some point during this phase, from organizational units wanting to sabotage the process to protect themselves, to those seeking to put themselves in positions to unfairly benefit from changes, to the unintended consequences of well-meaning supporters of change simply making mistakes along the way.

The change committee will need to remember its role in maintaining consensus as the foundation for future support throughout the organization. To do this, it will likely need to keep some problem statements more conceptual than specific at this stage, since the tendency of the IRS would almost certainly be to gravitate toward specifics managed through a detailed process with many steps and forms to complete along the way.

Many will attack remaining conceptual and focused on big problem statements at this stage, and their criticism will sound "right" in many cases.

"How can you solve a problem if you can't describe it in detail?" "Who caused the problem in the first place," and "Why would we trust that individual or organizational unit with the responsibility for solving a problem they created?"

In addition to these sorts of objections, I predict this complaint will come up early and often in the change process: "You just don't understand the way the IRS works."

At this stage of the process, the change committee will need to play a role to set the stage for success or failure. It must stay focused, honest, and transparent. It must be inclusive of everyone, even the people bringing these objections to the process. And it must work with senior management, marketing consultants, and the employees and taxpayers it represents to keep things moving forward. Ironically, in order to ensure the success of future actions, the committee will need to resist the temptation to start planning any actions. Its primary roles at this stage are to produce a report that builds consensus, and to do its best to make sure this consensus doesn't dilute the findings of the previous phase's market research.

Staying true to those findings while maintaining consensus is a tall order. The committee should feel comfortable taking the time it needs to complete this phase of the work, and to engage with people necessary to make real contributions. Time will also be needed to engage with other people who might be drifting away from the team because they think the problems are being defined in a way that makes them less comfortable, or who think the process is taking too long, or who are losing confidence that the process will succeed. They will need help, maybe from additional communications experts and even organizational experts who have experience managing change in large organizations. There will be challenges, maybe even big challenges, as the fact-finding report is assembled, distributed for review, and debated by participating stakeholders.

The change committee will need to work with an unwavering focus on its two goals: stay true to the facts revealed by the research, and maintain a foundation of consensus. If they can succeed in this this critical phase, they will have contributed more to the success of the transformation of the IRS than they will ever be recognized for delivering. But it will be worth it. And we all need to give them all the time and support they need.

Step Two: Bringing the Facts to All Constituencies

The challenges noted above are numerous, and in some cases, difficult to surmount. These difficulties are an inevitable result of moving from broad, conceptual, consensus-based process goals to the review and reporting of research results. It's impossible to go through this part of the process without someone's ox being gored. The prioritization of solvable problems could be avoided in the first phase of the project, where it was good enough to simply design a process to identify the problems every constituent might believe needs to be solved. But now it's time to list those problems, and decide which ones are most "popular," or—in market research terms—most widely reported.

How do we change from a process that avoids prioritization as a strategy for maintaining consensus, to a phase that requires prioritization? Can we do it without destroying the consensus built in the first phase of our work? While there is no foolproof answer, in my opinion there is at least a viable strategy for success. I like to call it "consensus-based prioritization."

Maybe I should have been a politician after all. But the term does, in fact, have real meaning. It means looking at the problems most often identified by participants in our market research, and reviewing these "popular" problems in several ways. First, we can look at them in terms of which can be solved with a minimal amount of opposition. The fact that the IRS needs a new computer system, for example, is a fairly safe problem to identify. While it might require a significant investment of money, software development, and employee training, few people with a serious interest in reforming the IRS would agree to a plan that doesn't address this issue. Another one might be the need to improve the IRS systems to be "responsive" to taxpayers wanting to request information or discuss a concern about individual tax liabilities, deductions, or other concerns. Who would seriously argue with the fact that a "courtesy hang up" is truly not courteous at all?

Another way to review these problems is to view them in terms of which functional IRS departments or regions would be affected by the selection of a solvable problem. If a way exists to distribute the impact of change so that no department or region is obviously affected more or less than other departments or regions, consensus may be maintained even as serious reforms are planned.

A third way is to be as neutral as possible in selecting solvable problems from the larger universe of problems identified by research. Avoiding any sort of priority order among those selected is one way of implementing this neutral point of view. In a sense, research results can be seen as providing a list of problems to solve on a kind of "pass/fail" basis. Problems are either selected for potential solution, or they're not. Once they're on the list, they're not prioritized in any other way. They can be listed as bullet points, or in alphabetical order, or in some other way, but not in any kind of list that implies one problem is more serious than another.

This same commitment to being neutral also applies to reporting of sources identifying problems selected by the change committee. Identifying a problem selected by business taxpayers, for example, or front-line IRS employees, could inadvertently create tension based on how other constituencies feel about these groups. And it would never be a good idea to identify the percentage of responders who isolated a problem for solution; this would certainly be a way to rank these problems by anyone who wanted to do so.

Finally, the change team might want to consider grouping related problems in the sense that solving them together might create a logical framework for future solution-oriented programs and actions. This is a tricky idea, since it might lead to groupings of problems that seem like assignment of blame to internal IRS constituencies or taxpayers in a way that makes these groups feel like they're being blamed for problems, igniting the organized opposition to the change process we're trying to avoid.

But if the problems tend to arrange themselves into "logical" structures solvable with a limited number of strategic change programs, rather than keeping separating each and requiring a change involving managing many individual change programs targeting a single problem, then grouping problems might be the way to go. I make no recommendation either way, since this decision can only be made at that point in the wonderful future when a change team is busily going gathering information about problems to solve, and maintaining the consensus necessary to solve them. With the appropriate warning included in this paragraph, we are once again at the point where all we can do is wish them the best and have faith that they will make the right decision.

Step Three: A Time for Compassion

In addition to considering all possible problems identified in the market research to select those the change team intends to solve; an equally important challenge arises at this stage of the process: the need to be compassionate and caring in dealing with the individuals whose careers will be affected by the changes as a consequence problem solving.

It's an unavoidable fact that not everyone's current job, or even their continued IRS employment, will be part of the agency's future as it reforms into a true customer service organization. Some functional departments will be phased out in favor of new staff structures, and technology may replace some clerical functions that are now the responsibility of IRS staff. Still other employees may be ill-suited the "new" customer-focused IRS, or may not have the time left in their careers to be re-trained and deployed in new department positions created by the change team's recommendations.

These people must be treated with respect and consideration for their service. It's as simple as that. Some management experts might say that it's important to treat them fairly as an example for those who remain in the new IRS, but that's not really the point. People deserve to be treated with compassion simply because they are people - they are not "examples" of the way others might be treated in the future. This sort of thinking diminishes all employees by treating them as teaching opportunities or research subjects for managerial initiatives, similar to how doctors once treated poor patients as research subjects to find cures for future patients at the expense of the research subjects.

It may seem odd for someone like me to say this, given some of the stories told about fellow employees and dysfunctional behavior in earlier chapters, but I truly believe that if we treat people well for their own sake, the examples we communicate to others will take care of themselves. But if we treat people in in ways to indirectly benefit future employee morale, or to create a false impression of compassion, our employees will eventually see through these practices for the manipulation they really are.

There are numerous specific programs the change team can recommend to handle altered or eliminated employees, so that those wishing to continue their IRS careers have the opportunity to do so, or at least apply for the chance to do so. They can remain in a position within their current department analogous to their current job, and be enrolled in training programs to add any new skills required. They can apply for transfer to another organizational unit where a job is available for someone with their skill level and experience, similar to the theoretical transfer opportunities in today's IRS. They can be given the opportunity to apply for advancement into new managerial positions through a "hire from within" program linked to the new structure that develops as the IRS transforms. Or they can apply for outplacement structured to be as generous and nonthreatening as possible for those who no longer fit into the new IRS. Gone will be the days of "leave and re-apply," in which current IRS employees must resign from their current jobs in order to submit an application for the new job they seek, risking unemployment if not hired.

Below are the values I believe the change team will include in this second phase of the change process:

- **Consensus**: the same value that needs to be included in all phases.
- **Credibility**: through their actions, members of the change team will demonstrate possession of credentials for which they were selected, as they make decisions about the problems to solve and communicate these decisions to all constituents in an ongoing dialogue.
- **Flexibility**: the change team will be willing to adjust its approach when necessary in order to maintain progress toward its overall goals, and to nurture the consensus so vital to its success.
- **Deliberation**: the change team will engage in its own dialogues in order to develop its list of problems to solve, and communicate its decisions with constituents in a way that shows the careful thought behind them.
- **Consideration (of consequences)**: the change team will engage in planning that anticipates potential outcomes of alternative courses of action before selecting the one they believe is best.
- **Compassion (for individual people)**: the change team will make every effort to treat all people involved in the process with respect and compassion for their own sake, and not simply to demonstrate good will to others not affected by these decisions.
- **Communication**: another of the two constant values throughout the process.

A Head Start on the Problems to Solve (Author's Perspective)

In my opinion, two key ways to face the challenges of this second phase developing new and improved training opportunities for IRS staff, and recruiting "change ambassadors" who can establish opportunities for dialogues about the change process with IRS employees, taxpayers, and other external constituents (for now, we will concentrate on the role these ambassadors will play inside the agency).

New and effective training opportunities would be linked to specific problems the change team selects, and the ways these plans create new jobs and career paths for future IRS employees. For example, current IT professionals might want to stay and be part of the new IRS information technology system, but in order to do so they must be re-trained to effectively implement, troubleshoot, and solve problems for the new hardware and software as the system begins full operations. Similar training for front-line customer service representatives involving protocols for taxpayer inquiries based on reforms in the way tax forms are designed, the automation of certain reporting requirements now done manually by both taxpayers and IRS staff, etc. And, if the change team agrees with my assessments, there will be no training programs involving long-distance flights and long hotel stays to draw in coloring books or sing songs required in the current IRS training programs.

Ambassadors would be people trained during the market research phase, so that they can address real concerns based on real responses from constituents participating in surveys. They might review these responses with the market research team and role-play dialogues with training staff to be more effective in their ambassadorial roles. These ambassadors can be volunteers from within the IRS, or they might be new specifically selected employees, depending on the change team's determination and its market research and communications consultants. In any case, the goals for these ambassadors would be to create real dialogues with IRS employees and managers as the change process develops, to answer their questions and report concerns back to the change team, followed by the replies from the change team to employees sharing these concerns. In this way, ambassadors will help a great deal in maintaining the consensus that is such an important part of the change process.

Ambassadors would encourage creativity and initiative among employees with whom they interact and, if the change committee decides to recruit these ambassadors from within the agency, this program would effectively reward employees who care about the agency and are willing to take risks in order to be part of the solution to the problems.

In addition, ambassador participation would in itself be a good way to encourage customer service and a problem-solving orientation among these ambassadors, who could then apply these skills to their current or new positions at the agency once the change process is complete. This would be a great way to demonstrate a clear alternative way to survive and thrive at the IRS besides the current, common "keep your head down" behavior.

CHAPTER

7

How to Do It, Part Three

THIS THIRD AND final phase of the process I recommend for reforming the IRS builds on the first two phases, and uses them as a foundation to launch a series of implementation plans for solving problems identified *by consensus* as those needing solutions. These individual phase plans will continue as parallel initiatives addressing each of the problems selected for solution, and will continue with the same values emphasized in the first two phases: maintaining consensus, being fact-based, supported by a flexible approach when better ideas surface, and further supported by a strong two-way communications effort bringing ideas from the change team to constituents, and ideas back from these constituents to the change team.

While this third phase is the last of the three "chapters" in reforming the IRS, and making it more customer service-focused, it is really a two-part initiative. The first part is internal to the IRS, and focuses on implementing a coordinated and parallel series of plans to solve identified problems This internal work requires an enormous managerial effort, since the progress of each of these parallel change efforts may at times be hindered by opposition from groups within the IRS opposing change. Change team managers must be quick to identify and solve problems as they pursue their work, and will need to maintain an overall consensus in ways that may be taxed (to coin a phrase) by the possibility of multiple resisting groups banding together to create a larger "leave us alone" effort.

Essentially, the change team's internal challenge will involve realistic managerial initiatives to solve problems like obsolete computers, antiquated policies and procedures, inadequate training of personnel, and misplaced energy by managers and the employees who work under them.

Implementing Internal Changes: The Need for Effective Communications

Their work will therefore also need to include communications and PR people continuously presenting the plan in a positive, nonthreatening, and inviting way for as many internal constituencies as possible. This communications team will meet with key stakeholders to review and confirm plans for solving problems and stress the likely benefits of achieving the change team's objectives. Tips on how to achieve these difficult goals can be found in our discussion of earlier phase priorities: the change team should focus on identifying phases of the change process as much as possible, avoiding talking about "priority areas" that might be seen as attacks on departments feeling criticized as "problem areas." It will still be important to avoid even the whiff of a blame game as much as possible, even though I believe, and so do many others within the IRS, that there is plenty of blame to go around.

The internal communications effort should be focused on making sure changes are seen as being organization-wide, as opposed to targeting specific units within the IRS. Goals should be keeping everybody involved, staying inclusive, emphasizing a team approach, and de-coupling discussions of problems from specific organizational units and people within the IRS. If possible, the change team and its communications representatives should focus their dialogues with IRS employees on overall goals, a project schedule for addressing change, and preparation for impending difficult choices by emphasizing a broad consensus for the coming changes.

This may be a time when the change process needs to slow down to focus on unifying themes such as improving customer service, obtaining new resources, and streamlining policies and procedures that will allow for more employee initiative and creativity. Above all, the change team will need to create opportunities for dialogue as much as possible, so employees feel engaged, involved, and able to influence the change process.

This will be a time when the change team must actively find and engage leaders within IRS stakeholder groups—representatives of management layers and organizational units who can work with the ambassadors developed in earlier phases, or perhaps become ambassadors for change themselves. To support these individuals, the change team may need to tailor communications to specific organizational units to allow supporters and ambassadors to deliver credible messages consistent with the overall goals of the change team. Group presentations and dialogues (as in new and improved "town hall meetings") may be in order, as will be training for these supporters, ambassadors, and even the employees with whom they are communicating, to demonstrate that the envisioned reforms are inclusive.

Internal changes will inevitably become concrete and specific at this stage of the process, and will therefore generate more contentious dialogue with those possible affected by the planned changes. There must be decisions about when to introduce the idea of early retirement, outplacement, or transfers to new departments or geographical regions, to the organizational units affected by substantially reducing or displacing current staff. This is where compassion comes into the process, along with a consistent focus on the benefits of a successful reform program. These concepts may seem simple in writing, but we can all agree that they will not be easy in practice. Still, they are essential to success.

It's Still a Beautiful World Outside of the IRS

At this stage, the change process is still in fact-finding mode for external stakeholders. While changes required inside the IRS are profound and will need time to process, taxpayers, tax preparers, and policy makers will be largely unaware of the internal change team's activities. They will still be evaluating and processing lists of solvable problems, and discussing these with the change team's external communications experts. While this may seem like a peaceful respite for change team members dealing with internal IRS opposition, this is in fact the time to shift the external dialogue from asking for changes, to reporting on changes under way inside the IRS. This reporting responsibility will also involve asking external constituents for thoughts and comments on the changes under way inside the IRS Their reactions will be valuable in identifying future communications programs aimed at external groups, but will also be useful in providing feedback to internal communicators who may want to inform IRS employees and management regarding what taxpayers, tax preparers, and policy makers think about the current changes.

This is also a time when progress may seem agonizingly slow, although there will be more than a few members of the change team welcoming the chance to focus on successfully completing each phase with each stakeholder group before moving on to the next. The cost is slow progress, but the benefit will be a reduced risk that the entire change process will be derailed by growing and unchallenged opposition.

The Public Relations/Communications Challenge

This final phase of the change process is when IRS communications consultants (who may be precursors to a full-fledged public relations department - see the next chapter) begin working on a comprehensive program informing external constituencies about the improvements being accomplished as the IRS transforms itself. The message to communicate will be tailored to fit the precise improvements and timetable in which they are rolled out, but the audiences will certainly include all the major taxpayer groups (individual, business/corporate, nonprofit, etc.), tax preparation organizations and accounting firms, and policy makers (government officials, consumer advocates, etc.). Another key audience will be the "change agents" the IRS will recruit to deliver the message to specific constituencies based on the trust change agents have established with their constituencies. This group can also be seen as external ambassadors, much like those recruited from within the IRS to champion the developing change process.

The IRS communications team will want to be sure that changes are presented as part of a consistent process that can be linked back to the earliest days of its existence. Facts discovered in the initial research phase should be used to justify initiatives as they begin, and particularly as they continue toward completion. This is perhaps the best way to ensure that opponents of the change gain control of the way external constituencies see the IRS reforms. It will be more difficult for them to do so if the IRS maintains that what is happening "today" at some point in the future is in fact part of a plan reviewed and approved months or even years before. Referencing the comprehensive nature of that planning process will be an important element in these communications programs, as will be a similar linking of everything—current initiatives and previous planning efforts—to the IRS mission. A final element in these messages can also be a look ahead to future progress as a stronger, more customer service-oriented, "new and improved" IRS evolves from the change team's master plan.

Techniques to help keep these messages consistent over time might include a standard timetable graphic with the entire change process mapped out, and frequent updates indicated by a "you are here" symbol to mark progress toward the ultimate goal. Another good idea for these communications would be honest reporting of how the change process is going. If everything proceeds according to plan, it will be important to share that good news, and distribute as much credit as possible to people outside of the immediate change team (remember my earlier prediction that a successful change process might have "too many winners").

On the other hand, if problems develop, it wouldn't hurt to admit them publicly, along with strategies for addressing these implementation problems as reported. Failing to discuss bad news is a hallmark of a dysfunctional organization, and several constituencies—both inside and outside the IRS—will be looking for signs that this sort of behavior is continuing despite the organization's commitment to change.

As the change process develops, the issue of who should be the "voice" of change will be an important consideration.

Initially, the change team will want to be visible in order to use its credentials to add credibility to the change process. At these early phases, it would be wise for IRS senior management to not be the primary communicators. This might be seen as evidence that nothing will change, since the "old" power structure is reporting on how new changes are coming. But at a certain point, the commitment of the organization as a whole becomes its own important message.

In my view, the time for this is at this final stage of the change process, when multiple parallel change programs are under way, and changes will begin to effect employees, taxpayers, and other outside constituents who interact with the IRS. Receiving communications from the most senior levels of the IRS as changes are happening will reinforce the idea that the process has the organization's full support, and that it's managed by people with credibility to be in charge of a process that might be difficult, time-consuming, or controversial, or expensive.

Another way to show full organizational support for the change process would be to use the media to get the story out. Regular IRS newsletters, video messages, blogs, press releases, and internal media should all be places to find updates about the changes. As a number of different and parallel change programs are under way, these media channels might help by featuring not only IRS senior leadership, but also different people involved in the change program. Giving internal and external constituencies the correct impression of a growing team of IRS change agents is a good idea, and this final phase of the program is when communicating this idea will be most helpful.

This will be true of current "change agents" and ambassadors, but featuring new individuals involved in growing change initiatives will be valuable as well. For example, the new information technology team hired to install a new IRS computer system would almost certainly be a popular group to feature in news stories about what is coming at the new, improved IRS.

There are three types of message themes to consider in telling the story of change at the IRS as it unfolds. The first is "we've done it," which includes reports of completed work to install new systems, launch new training programs, open a new and responsive customer service center, and update key parts of the tax code.

The second is "we've listened to you," a good way to report on work in progress. Talking about a process working toward a goal that everyone has already supported in earlier phases of the change program will remind everyone that things are moving forward according to plan, and that the plan is still the one they agreed to support.

A third way to communicate changes might be called, "watch this space." This approach is reserved for changes not yet in place, but will begin to be implemented once current work is completed. In this third theme, it will be important to tell a story that provides consistent links to past planning and current activity, to demonstrate that future changes might be "new," but they will not be unexpected.

In all three cases, it might make for good story-telling to include people in the messages who will add credibility to the story. For example, satisfied taxpayers who have had a positive experience with completed customer service programs, or the IT team as they install a new computer system. Working with these people as ambassadors will also mean making them available as part of a dialogue with constituencies receiving their messages. This interactivity will be its own message, and will add credibility to the story and win support from people who believe they are being heard.

Below are the values I believe the change team will include in this third phase of the change process:

- **Consensus:** Our old favorite, this can never be ignored. It will be most difficult in this phase, and yet also most important.
- **Leadership**: The change team must provide steady leadership and near-constant communication of its attention to all details of the complex changes being implemented in this phase. In addition, the team will need to delegate some of these leadership responsibilities to ambassadors, change agents, and its communications team, requiring its own style of visionary leadership and management.
- **Implementation:** This is the phase when work gets done. Generalized and conceptual plans are increasingly replaced by action-oriented programs, monitoring of progress, and necessary adjustments. Dealing with opposition is included in my definition of "implementation," because this is when those resistant to change will be the most motivated to disrupt the process. Some may argue that this is in fact "leadership," which is fine by me, as long as it happens in this critical phase.
- **Perspective:** The change team will do well to remember its past work and the value of the foundations built in the earliest phases. This will be the time to withdraw from accounts of good will, and rely on the fact that there is enough in these accounts to sustain the process in its crucial phases. Risks include: dealing with opposition, running out of resources, responding

to unexpected flaws in systems and procedures as they come online. But perhaps the best perspective will be to remember the importance of priorities—something I recommended the change team downplay in early phases, but a concept that will be critical as the process nears completion. As multiple parallel change programs advance, it will be valuable to consider which are most important, so if one or more bogs down, the existence of this problem by itself is not the only factor to consider in possible redirection of energy and resources. If the flailing change program is critically important, by all means do whatever is necessary to get it back on track. However, if it's a minor change, it might be best to let it lie briefly while more important changes continue to receive the support as planned.

- **Vision (for the long haul):** There will be enormous temptation to get lost in the weeds at this stage of the process. Problems will arise on a frequent basis. Suggestions for improvements or customization of previously-approved programs will be rampant. Communications people will demand information to maintain the continued support of key constituencies, inside and outside of the IRS. The change team cannot ignore these events, and is correct in paying attention to them as much as possible. But like the prioritization noted above in "perspective," anything that distracts the overall change process from its ultimate goal of a transformed IRS that successfully fulfills its mission and reinvents itself as a customer service-driven organization should always play second fiddle to that vision.

- **Communication:** This second old friend, like "consensus," will continue to be a primary value throughout the change process. And like our other old friend, it will be most demanding in this final phase. Constant communication with multiple constituencies will be vital to success.

A Head Start on the Problems to Solve (Author's Perspective)

I am of two minds when thinking of this third and final phase of the change process. First, it is the most difficult of times in trying to transform the IRS, since real work must be done, real choices need to be made, and real opposition is likely to be encountered as the change team tries to do its job. On the other hand, it is also an exciting prospect for me, because it means that the agency will be closer than it has ever been to actually becoming an efficient, customer service-driven organization. There are a few thoughts to share that might help increase the chances of success at this stage.

First, make sure that the change team maintains its attention to detail and solid dialogue with people in all constituencies. There can be no "hidden agendas," yet some seemingly cooperative individuals may in try to camouflage their sabotage. The change team should be ever-vigilant to warning signs that things might be coming off the rails based on their own observations and evaluation criteria, and not lose sight of the programs' overall progress by over-delegating. Delegating work will be essential, but delegating quality control is rarely worth the risk—even though it saves precious time and energy. Now is not the time to rest on past accomplishments. If the change team needs more resources to maintain its quality control responsibilities, these should be resources it controls.

The change team should also try to keep various strategies for getting things back on track in its "hip pockets." Knowing where problems are likely to occur is a valuable resource, because it allows the team to brainstorm possible solutions for problems before they occur. Nothing will ever go completely according to plan, of course, and this is particularly true when managers try to anticipate problems and build solutions on those anticipations. Still, with some flexibility, a framework for solving likely problems may help the team intervene quickly and decisively while it considers more targeted, specific solutions.

Finally, I would remind the change team of how a tried-and-true conceptual disclaimer applies to this phase of the process: "It's a work in process." Changing the IRS will be difficult. There is no guarantee of success. But there will always be something that can be done to make things better than they are—today, on that day in the future when the change process begins, and in those most trying days in the final phase of the process when everything happens at once and success seems so near and yet so far. I'm very excited about the prospect of successful change at the IRS and hope to see it happen.

CHAPTER

8

Conclusion—What I Would Do

In order to wrap up this book, I believe I owe the reader two things: first, I want to recap in short, bullet-point format, the three major categories of problems that I've experienced from inside the IRS. Second, I want to repeat my belief in the fact-based, deliberate, consensus-driven change process I've outlined in chapters four through seven of this book; and third, I want to offer my own recommendations for changes I would want to see as a result of this process.

The problems at the IRS: Three big categories.

Without going into details, remember that the problems at the IRS can be viewed in these three categories:

1. The Tax Code. It is antiquated, difficult to understand, and has evolved into a system unfairly serving wealthy and powerful taxpayers who can afford to hire lawyers and other consultants to avoid their responsibility to pay taxes through numerous loopholes that have developed over time.

2. Resource Starvation. Through a series of budget reductions, the IRS has become an organization with fewer employees than it has had in previous years, yet these professionals are doing more work than ever before. In addition, there are no funds available to upgrade antiquated computer systems, policies, and procedures that need to be modernized.
3. A Dysfunctional Staff and Management Structure. The organization has become top-heavy with nine layers of seniority, and a system for communicating that emphasizes top-down managerial direction without the opportunity for any bottom-up feedback. Work has become the preparation of a seemingly endless series of reports, along with meaningless and wasteful staff conferences and training sessions, coupled with an inability or unwillingness to remove employees and managers who are performing poorly. The result is a brain drain of good employees and frustration for those who remain and want to do a good job.

The change process: Why it needs to be deliberate and consensus-based.

To reform any large organization, particularly one as large and dysfunctional as the IRS, you need to approach the challenge with both perspectives. You need to know the problems, and you need to approach solving them in a way that won't be distracted by the myriad of small issues that can stand in the way of progress. I think the solution I've proposed is a wise one, precisely because it focuses on a fair process rather than specific recommendations. As I've written earlier, any list of specific recommendations for reforming the IRS is nothing more than a bulls-eye for target practice by constituencies resistant to change. That is why I have resisted them. Until now.

My Solutions to the Problems at the IRS

As promised, I am happy to offer the following outline of solutions I would recommend for reforming the IRS and making a successful, customer service-oriented organization. Chief among these are:

- Implement better hiring **practices**. We need to recruit the best talent possible, and orient them to the realities of working at the IRS. Hiring qualified people is something that can be outsourced—human resources professionals can help with this part of the challenge. What is needed in addition is an orientation process to eliminate the kind of surprises I found after landing my job—the paperwork, politics, and antiquated policies and procedures I would face as part of my job. Ideally, a reformed IRS at some point in the future won't need to disclose these issues to new employees. But today, in order to recruit people who understand the challenges they will face, more honesty will be important.
- **Encourage and train employees and managers to resolve tax controversies at the lowest level possible.** This is a value that can be instilled early in an employee's career, and it can serve both the individual and the organization well. Solving problems at the lowest level possible empowers

IRS employees and encourages skill development, creativity, and problem-solving skills. It also builds professionalism, teamwork, and morale. There is no reason to kick everything upstairs. A simple commitment to solve problems in direct interactions with taxpayers is another way to make the IRS a more successful customer service organization.

- **Remove poor performing front-line employees and managers**. This is always a difficult challenge when reforming a large, dysfunctional organization. There are many people currently employed by the IRS who probably won't be part of a new and successful agency. They may not make the grade, but they are still human beings, and many of them have dedicated years if not decades to the IRS. We need to provide incentives for them to leave voluntarily, by offering buyouts, severance packages, early retirement, and other programs to encourage them to move on with their pride and sense of self-worth intact. Not fitting into the new IRS is not the worst thing in the world, and we should never make anyone feel like it is.
- **Remove under-performing senior managers and executives**. This same commitment to making it as painless as possible to move on from the IRS is as important for managers as it is for employees. It also may be necessary to remove senior managers simply because the current IRS is management-heavy. There is no need for the large number of people in these positions in a successful customer service organization. Flattening out the organization structure will eliminate needless lay-

ers of management and support problem solving at the lowest possible level of the organization, as mentioned above.

- **Change the culture and mentality of the organization**. Emphasize customer service, encourage a can-do attitude, remove political savvy as a core competency, implement modern management and motivation techniques, and provide people with the resources they need to do their jobs.
- **Create a public relations department to repair the public image of the IRS**. Why not? As we work to reform the IRS, it will be important to let taxpayers know what we're doing. A public relations function—eventually an internal communications department, but initially perhaps a public relations consulting firm—is a great way to inform people about the changes being made at the IRS, and the benefits these changes will bring to them.

Closing Thoughts from a Lifetime IRS Employee

Yes, Virginia, that's me. I can't lie and say that sometimes my work at the IRS has (not) been extremely frustrating. Not only have I experienced conflict with fellow employees and confronted people I believe are doing less than possible to make the agency work as intended, I have also been reprimanded and disciplined for some of these sincere efforts. But overall, I believe in the mission of the organization, and look forward to the day when the IRS will proudly practice its mission "to provide America's taxpayers top quality service by helping them understand and meet their tax responsibilities and by applying the tax law with integrity and fairness to all."

The problems I have described in this book are real, but they are surmountable. The process I have outlined for future IRS reform is long and perhaps tedious, but it will succeed. The changes I believe will make the agency a truly successful customer service organization are difficult, but achievable. Big changes begin at the grass-roots level. Perhaps successful reform of the IRS will begin with the ideas of an employee who believes in the power of individual, bottom-up hard work.

If I were in charge of reforming the agency, I would have begun the change process outlined in this book long ago. But because I'm realistic in terms of how long it will take to even begin this reform process, let alone how long it will take, I believe that my recommendations might be old news or perhaps even ancient history by the time the change process is underway. I have purposely left them out of the "How to Do It" chapters, because there's no telling what the real problems with the IRS will be when the change process actually begins. However, since I believe it would be a grave disappointment for me to not include my own ideas, I have saved them for this concluding chapter, where they can be presented with the proper disclaimer that they may not apply when the IRS is finally reformed.

Finally, I want readers to know that, since I began writing this book, I have reluctantly decided to retire from the IRS. It's time for me to move on, and to enjoy the rest of my life without the stress and frustrations I have described herein. But I have not given up the fight to change the organization to which I have dedicated my career, nor have I given up hope that these changes are truly possible. They may be the responsibility of future employees and leaders at the IRS instead of myself and my colleagues, but they are still necessary and will, in my opinion, one day come to pass. My commitment to inspiring these changes has been expressed in two ways: first, I have written this book for everyone to read and evaluate for themselves whether, and how, to change the IRS for the better. Second, I have written a lengthy letter of resignation, outlining the problems I have experienced and describing some of the ways I think they can be solved.

That letter, which will include several sections readers of this book will find familiar, is included as an Appendix to this book. I hope my experiences, recommendations, perspective, and ideas will be helpful to the people who will take on the vital challenge of reforming the IRS by taking a marketing approach to the challenge, creating an agency that is truly customer service oriented, and dedicated to its mission.

Appendix: My Letter to the IRS

The Internal Revenue Service's mission is to provide America's taxpayers with top-quality service by helping them understand and meet their tax responsibilities and enforce tax laws with integrity and fairness for all.

However, we at the IRS are failing at our mission because we do not provide the American taxpayer with top-quality service. In fact, I would argue that we do just the opposite: provide extremely poor service.

We do not help taxpayers understand and meet their obligations, and we do not enforce tax laws with integrity and fairness for all. I have broken down into three broad categories the reasons why we are failing at our mission:

1. The Tax Code and the Administration of the Tax System
2. Lack of Resources/Resource Starvation
3. IRS Culture, Practices, and Systems

1. The Tax Code and the Administration of the Tax System

A. The tax code is overly complex. If you have tried to lift the printed Internal Revenue Code and accompanying regulations recently, you know what

I am talking about. You literally could hurt your back.

B. The tax code is poorly written, i.e., difficult to read and understand. Even IRS experts have a difficult time understanding and interpreting the code, so what hope is there for the average U.S. taxpayer?

C. The tax code is outdated. The code has not been revised significantly since 1986, during the Reagan administration.

D. The tax code is biased/unfair. The code heavily favors the upper class/wealthy taxpayers (top 1%) over lower- and middle-class taxpayers (bottom 99%) by allowing for:

- Corporate inversions
- Preferential tax treatment for certain types of income, such as capital gains and stock dividends
- Tax-exempt status for interest received from municipal bonds
- Favorable deductions for owners of rental real estate.
- Flow-through entities such as partnerships and S-corporations. My experience has been that partnerships and S-corporations are breeding grounds for tax avoidance/evasion. Trying to find income within them often is like playing "Where's Waldo?"

The wealthy often can get around paying their taxes. Wealthy taxpayers hire CPAs, attorneys, etc., to protect them. Often, they simply wear us down because we do not have the resources to keep up with them. We cannot possibly take every case to tax court because we simply do not have the resources. Over and over again, I have seen wealthy taxpayers paying as much as or more to their CPAs and attorneys than what they would have if they had just paid the tax liabilities they challenged. Lower- and middle-class taxpayers do not have the resources to hire this kind of representation and often simply wind up paying what they owe.

Gaming or rigging the system is possible. The XYZ group specializes in helping taxpayers (generally wealthy business owners) find deductions/loopholes in the code as it pertains to research credits, and the company is very aggressive in its approach. In my opinion, the XYZ group often helps its clients evade taxes, and the IRS currently is conducting a preparer project on the company. In other words, the XYZ group is a bad apple/thorn in the IRS' side. Three former IRS commissioners are board members at the XYZ group. I can understand IRS executives returning to the private sector, but heading a firm that is aggressively promoting questionable tax avoidance/evasion strategies? Why hasn't this fact been more publicized? I would think that the general public/American taxpayers would be outraged at this. This is the equivalent of law enforcement officials leaving government service, then joining criminal groups for lucrative salaries.

The above practices result in wealthy taxpayers paying less than their proportionate share of tax. For example, billionaire Berkshire Hathaway Chairman Warren Buffett paid 17% in tax, and former presidential candidate and businessman Mitt

Romney paid 11% in tax. These are lower percentages than what I pay. I am a GS-14 front-line government employee. Why am I paying a higher proportionate share of taxes than billionaires? We need to adjust the system.

2) Lack of Resources/Resource Starvation

A. The IRS computer systems are outdated. I estimate that our technology is approximately 20 years behind what is currently being used in the private sector, which puts IRS employees and managers at a huge disadvantage in terms of productivity. We are less-efficient than what we would be otherwise. I can't imagine how much time is wasted because of this.

B. The IRS is facing severe attrition, as it has not been able to hire new employees for years because of budget constraints and a hiring freeze in effect since 2010. In 2002, when I joined the IRS, the agency employed approximately 125,000 people. Currently, the IRS employs approximately 88,000, a 30 percent workforce reduction in 15 years. Considering the IRS workload has increased during this period, it has been forced to do more with less.

C. The IRS faces an attrition crisis due to aging workers. A considerable percentage of the agency's workforce currently is eligible for retirement, including 41% of front-line managers, an ongoing concern for the agency.

D. The IRS does not have an effective succession plan in place to replace retiring workers. This creates what is commonly referred to as "brain drain" as the agency loses experienced people at a steady pace due to attrition. However, it cannot replace them with new people because of the hiring freeze. Furthermore, fewer experienced people are available to train newer hires.

3) IRS Culture, Practices, and Systems

A. The management philosophy is outdated, based on military culture, with a top-down mentality: Respect the chain of command and follow orders. Do not question authority or ask why an order is given, or even if it makes sense—just blindly obey it. Follow that order because you were told to, or because that is the way it always has been done. This mentality creates "yes" people, rendering the agency less effective.

B. The IRS has too many procedures. These procedures are cumbersome, constantly changing, and further convoluted—much like the tax code—by individual interpretation therein, depending on your particular supervisor. This creates an immense amount of frustration and confusion among employees. There is a saying at the IRS: Don't bother to learn the new procedure because it will change again shortly.

C. There is an extreme amount of manager turnover at all levels at the IRS. I have had nine different direct supervisors during my IRS career. Such constant change in supervisors is disheartening, creating inconsistency that takes a heavy toll on continuity, teamwork, individual effort, and overall morale.

D. The IRS constantly is realigning its management structure. Currently, I am going through a realignment in my business unit (Office of Appeals). I recently left SBSE-Exam, which also went through a recent realignment. I must say that the SBSE-Exam realignment (Northern California merging with the Western Area) was one of the worst experiences of my 30-plus-year professional career. The way that particular realignment was handled was awful. The IRS executive in charge of it should have been fired. However, in true IRS form, that particular executive received a promotion. Sounds crazy, but it is actually quite common at the IRS for people to get promoted for terrible work. The constant realigning of management structure and the high manager turnover create lots of stress, frustration, and confusion among front-line employees and managers.

E. The front-line manager job at the IRS is an awful job, and employees know it. Therefore, the best and brightest generally do not choose management as a career path. The best and brightest should be pursuing promotions to management so that the organization can thrive, but they know what a thankless and stressful job being a front-line manager can be. As a front-line manager, you have all the responsibility without any power. You essentially do not have the authority to hire and fire people. You inherit a team of employees and must do the best you can with them. If you inherit a team that includes incompetent or mediocre employees, you essentially are stuck with those employees. Removing a poor-performing employee once he or she gets past the probationary period is an extremely difficult thing to do at the IRS. I went through the removal/firing process with one employee, and I wound up in the hospital for a brief period because the stress was overwhelming. This reminds me of a saying from one of my favorite former football coaches, Bill Parcells, who said the following when he resigned from a particular team: "If you are going to ask me to cook the meal, then you should at least let me shop for the ingredients."

F. There is a lack of leadership at the IRS. Several employees feel helpless. I have heard it described frequently as being a rudderless ship in the middle of the ocean, or the Titanic before it hits the iceberg.

G. The IRS provides horrible customer service to both its internal and external customers. If you have ever tried to call the IRS help line, you know what I am talking about. It is embarrassing for me to be part of an organization that provides this level of customer service. The fact that we engage in something called a "Courtesy Hang-Up" says it all. If a private company provided that kind of customer service, it would go out of business quickly. Such service simply would not be tolerated in the private sector.

H. Too much internal reporting/documenting is required by employees and managers. One reason why I chose accounting as my profession is because I do not enjoy writing. Had I enjoyed or had a passion for writing, I would have become a journalist, author, English teacher, etc. No one told me when I joined the IRS that I would be writing so much. At the IRS, writing reports is an Olympic event. It's as if we worship internal reports and documents. I worked in the private sector for 20 years before I joined the IRS, and I honestly can say that I spent little or no time preparing reports for internal purposes. In the private sector, companies are concerned with making a profit. Therefore, writing internal reports generally is not a high priority for its front-line employees and managers. It is my experience that the internal reports we prepare add little or no value to the agency's overall mission. I can't for the life of me understand why the IRS requires so many internal reports. It defies logic and is very inefficient. A great deal of time is wasted that could be used much more productively. I will provide two examples to illustrate my point. The first is from the front-line employee's point of view and the second is from the front-line manager's point of view.

I was a revenue agent in the SBSE-Exam business unit from 2002 through 2008. I would go out into the field to conduct audits. I generally arrived at 9 a.m. at wherever I was sent. I would meet with the taxpayer(s) and/or taxpayer representative(s), conduct an initial interview, review the books and records, make an audit determination, and issue the report. Hopefully, all of that would happen in one or two days. The taxpayer(s) and/or representative(s) would sign the audit report and pay all or part of the tax liability, if there was one. However, I then would need to spend the next three or four days documenting, organizing, indexing, and assembling the case file. How effective is this process? One or two days to conduct the audit/assess the liability and three or four days to document the case file? The auditor should only be required to document the case file thoroughly if the taxpayer does not agree with the auditor's ruling, and the case might go to Appeals and/or Tax Court. If the taxpayer agrees with the decision, why are we spending all this time producing detailed reports for internal purposes? The taxpayer and/or the representative will never see these reports that we create. They are for our internal purposes only. I estimate that I worked and closed over 200 cases during my time as a revenue agent. Could you imagine how many cases I could have closed if there had been no unnecessary burdensome internal reporting requirements, for cases that truly did not need them? I believe I could have closed twice as many cases in that same time frame. I would have been twice as productive. I believe I would have closed 400 cases during those six years. I also would have enjoyed the job more because I would have been doing what I liked doing—working with taxpayers and representatives to resolve tax discrepancies rather than typing and assembling reports. During my time as a revenue agent, I estimate that approximately 20% of my time was spent conducting audits. The other 80% was spent doing busy work that does not further our mission.

I currently supervise an employee who is about as good an employee as you could ever want—outstanding in every sense of the word. She has a 5.0 rating, the highest possible at the IRS. I am required, as a front-line manager, to prepare 10 written evaluations/reviews for this employee annually: at least seven case reviews, one workload review, one mid-year review, and one annual appraisal. Each review/evaluation is the equivalent of writing a mini-term paper. I want to highlight two things: This is the bare minimum expected from me as her direct supervisor, and this is for only one employee. The average supervisory load for a front-line manager in the IRS is 10 employees. I estimate that it takes me approximately 50 hours to prepare those 10 reviews/evaluations. Multiply that by 10 employees, and you are now talking about 500 hours per year devoted to written employee-evaluation feedback. Why in the world would employees need that much written feedback? I work with the aforementioned employee daily, continually telling her how much I value and appreciate her hard work. I have spoken to her, and she could care less about receiving the feedback. How many different ways can I write about what a great job she is doing? In the private sector, I worked for both large and small firms, and I never once received written feedback. I would receive verbal feedback, and everyone was fine with that. Now, if you add in the other reporting requirements of an IRS front-line manager, such as monthly reports, quarterly briefings, annual operation reviews, ad hoc reports, etc., I would estimate that easily 40% to 50% of a front-line manager's time is spent preparing internal reports and documents.

I. There are too many internal meetings and conferences. If report writing is an Olympic event at the IRS, attending internal meetings and conferences is at least a junior Olympic event. The IRS loves meetings and conferences almost as much as it loves reports. I estimate that approximately 150 hours per year of a front-line manager's time is spent attending internal meetings and conferences. This means almost 10% of an IRS front-line manager's time is spent attending meetings and conferences.

Let's recap. I have demonstrated that over 50% of a front-line manager's time is spent writing internal reports and attending internal meetings/conferences. Now we need to factor in mandatory training, briefings, continuing education, special projects, etc. I would estimate that this takes up another 100 to 200 hours per year. Therefore, I could easily make the case that somewhere between 50% to 75% of a front-line manager's time is accounted for before he or she does anything even resembling what we would normally think of in terms of running a team. This means 50% to 75% of a front-line manager's time is taken before he or she does any of the following: assign work, close cases, conduct informal reviews/discussions, manage workloads, conduct inventory, manage workflow, develop and motivate employees, self-development, internal/external outreach, taxpayer/representative conferences (closing conferences), labor-relations issues, troubleshooting problems, conducting research, etc. Is it any wonder why the front-line manager position is not highly sought after within the IRS?

J. There are too many executives/levels of management. There are seven levels of management between a revenue agent and the top executive in the Small Business/Self-Employed business unit. That is simply too many levels of management. It becomes a game of telephone trying to deliver messages from the SBSE-Commissioner (top executive) to revenue agents (front-line employees). Two sayings apply here: "Too many cooks spoil the broth" and "Too many chiefs and not enough Indians."

K. There is no effective two-way communication. Messages are sent from the top down, but not sent or considered from the bottom up. Honest feedback from front-line employees and managers is discouraged. I will provide an example: The IRS commissioner held a town hall meeting for front-line managers in March 2016. I attended the meeting and asked a question during the Q&A session. I stated many of the issues/problems that IRS front-line managers face. I asked how the front-line manager's job could be made easier, i.e., how could the managerial burden be reduced? I stated my question and comments clearly, calmly, and professionally, and they sparked a good, healthy dialogue. One of the executives on the panel actually said he agreed with my comments and thanked me for speaking up. The meeting went well, and I was glad that I attended and participated. After the meeting, I received many positive comments from fellow front-line managers. I also received calls and e-mails over the next few days, saying I did good by speaking up on behalf of front-line managers and addressing these concerns. However, not all the feedback I received was positive. Senior manager(s) received word about my comments and took those comments personally. Senior manager(s) contacted my direct supervisor and asked that I be disciplined/reprimanded for my insubordinate comments. Luckily for me, my direct supervisor didn't cave in regarding this request and conducted due diligence on the issue. My direct supervisor made inquiries and discovered that I had, in fact, done nothing wrong. So much for providing honest feedback. I have found during my 15 years at the IRS that upper management says they welcome or encourage honest feedback, but they really don't. This is just lip service. They welcome feedback only when it is positive. They do not want to hear negative feedback or anything that even resembles constructive criticism.

L. A pass-the-buck mentality exists at the IRS. If writing reports and attending meetings are Olympic events, passing the buck must be at least a national amateur tournament. IRS employees and managers receive work and often reject it or return it to the sender. It is as if people within the IRS actually derive pleasure from rejecting work and telling you the reasons why they are not required to do the work. The employee or manager then will state the reason(s) for rejecting the work, e.g., because a form was missing or wasn't completed properly, or it wasn't the most updated version of the form, or that a procedure wasn't followed properly, etc. If feels like some employees and managers at the IRS spend more time and effort getting out of doing work than actually doing work. However, we do a whole lot of unnecessary package shipping. There is so much waste in terms of how often we ship packages back and forth. It seems like we keep UPS, FedEx, and the USPS in business singlehandedly.

M. There are too many poor- and mediocre-performing employees. There are lower-level employees and managers working at the IRS whom I truly believe would not be able to work in the private sector. These employees and managers have become governmentalized from working here, or else they didn't have the skills to begin with when we hired them. We have many lower-level employees and managers who would not be tolerated in the private sector, where they could and would be fired "at will." Employees can't be fired "at will" at the IRS. Like I said earlier, it is very difficult to remove poor-performing employees at the IRS. Many of them game the system because of this.

N. There is a micromanaging mentality at the IRS. I was never micromanaged in the private sector, where either you performed, or you would need to look for a new job. I was given assignments, then left alone to complete them. At the IRS, we micromanage routinely. I do not like to micromanage people, and I, in turn, do not like to be micromanaged. Consequently, I refuse to micromanage my employees, which often puts me at odds with senior managers and executives who believe in micromanaging. Many senior managers and executives at the IRS are lifetime federal government employees, so micromanaging is the only way they know how to operate.

O. Management is often dishonest. I can't tell you how many times I have had senior managers and fellow front-line managers say to me the following: "Wow, I can't believe that you told your employees that/that you shared that with them." The bottom line is that I tell my employees everything. If I know it, they know it. This practice of keeping information from front-line employees is something I really don't understand. Over and over again, I have seen managers at all levels withhold information from employees, telling half-truths or straight-up lying to their employees. I don't play that game. I am direct and honest with my employees. They know the good and the bad at all times. I believe people appreciate when you are direct/honest/straight with them.

P. Political savvy actually is a core competency at the IRS. Managers at all levels actually are reviewed and graded on how well they practice political savvy. Needless to say, I always fail in this category. I am terrible at political savvy because I despise it. However, it is very important at the IRS—possibly even more important than knowledge and skills. I know quite a few people who have gone far in this organization because they are good at political savvy, i.e., office politics. I wouldn't even know how to play the political game if I wanted to do so. I am direct and honest to a fault. It is the only way I know, and the only way I have ever known how to operate. I believe you should rise or fall based on your merits. I obviously am naïve, and I have been told over and over again the following by IRS managers: "Phil, you are smart, talented, and have a lot going for you, but you are never going to get anywhere in this organization because of your lack of political savvy. You ruffle people's feathers, and people don't appreciate that. You speak out too much. Sometimes, it is better to just shut your mouth and go along to get along." I can tell you right now that I will never do that. Life is too short, and money and position aren't important enough for me to compromise my principles. To me, political savvy is another way of saying, "Kiss ass and don't make waves." I'm not interested in self-preservation. I'm interested in doing what's right, period. I'm interested in effecting change in a positive way.

Q. The IRS has an ineffective system for measuring business results concerning both quality and quantity.

R. The IRS has unfair promotional practices. Far too often, receiving a promotion in this organization has nothing to do with your competency in the position. This is where political savvy comes into play. Politics has a huge bearing on who receives a promotion, especially at the management level.

S. It is far too difficult to remove or demote poor-performing employees.

T. People are not utilized properly in this organization. I will use myself as an example. I am bright, talented, and have outstanding people skills. I am excellent at motivating people, giving speeches, selling ideas, resolving controversies, and negotiating settlements. However, my skills are not utilized at the IRS. I have been a front-line manager for the past eight years, stuck behind a computer typing meaningless internal reports (checking boxes). I previously have applied for positions in this organization both in stakeholder relations and in public affairs/public relations. I was turned down both times. You mean to tell me that there are people in this organization who are better suited for these positions than I am? If there are, I truly want to meet them and tip my hat to them. I have a hard time believing that. There is often no rhyme or reason to how people receive positions/promotions at the IRS.

U. An employee's annual rating often has no bearing on how well that employee performs his or her job. I have seen employees rated 3.6 or below who were excellent at what they do. Conversely, I have seen employees rated 4.6 or above who were awful at their job. The annual ratings given by this organization are often not worth the paper on which they are printed.

Made in the USA
Monee, IL
04 November 2026

67386410R10095